Y0-EHI-322

¡BUEN VIAJE!
TEACHER'S MANUAL

Jo Anne Wilson
Educational Consultant

Jacqueline Moase-Burke
Oakland Schools
Waterford, Michigan

Prentice Hall

A Pearson Education Company
Upper Saddle River, New Jersey 07458

Copyright © 1994 by Pearson Education, Inc., publishing as Prentice Hall, Upper Saddle River, New Jersey 07458. All rights reserved. Printed in the United States of America. This publication is protected by copyright, and permission should be obtained from the publisher prior to any prohibited reproduction, storage in a retrieval system, or transmission in any form or by any means, electronic, mechanical, photocopying, recording, or likewise. For information regarding permission(s), write to: Rights and Permissions Department.

ISBN 0-8384-4935-2

5 6 7 8 9 10   05 04 03 02

CONTENTS

WHAT IS AN EXPLORATORY COURSE?   V

TO THE TEACHER   VI

    THE ADOLESCENT/PRE-ADOLESCENT LEARNER   VI

    BUILDING LANGUAGE SKILLS IN THE FLEX CLASSROOM   VIII

    BUILDING CULTURAL AWARENESS IN THE FLEX CLASSROOM   X

    TEACHING STRATEGIES FOR THE FLEX CLASSROOM   XI

    UTILIZING TECHNOLOGY IN THE FOREIGN LANGUAGE CLASSROOM   XII

    ASSESSMENT AND EVALUATION   XIII

    HOW TO USE THE ELEMENTS: AN OVERVIEW   XV

ELEMENT 1   LEARNING ABOUT HOMESTAY COUNTRIES, CITIES, AND LANGUAGES   1

ELEMENT 2   PACKING   11

ELEMENT 3   TRIP PLANS   21

ELEMENT 4   TRAVEL DETAILS   31

ELEMENT 5   EXCHANGING LETTERS WITH YOUR HOST FAMILY   39

ELEMENT 6   PREPARING A PHOTO ALBUM   47

ELEMENT 7   ARRIVAL   51

ELEMENT 8   YOUR HOMESTAY HOUSE AND DAILY ROUTINE   57

ELEMENT 9   GETTING AROUND TOWN   67

ELEMENT 10   **GOING TO SCHOOL IN YOUR HOMESTAY COUNTRY**   79

ELEMENT 11   **SIGHTSEEING**   87

ELEMENT 12   **A BIRTHDAY PARTY**   97

ELEMENT 13   **RECUERDOS DE UN BUEN VIAJE**   107

WHAT IS AN EXPLORATORY COURSE?

The Foreign Language Exploratory Course or Foreign Language Experience is frequently referred to by the acronym FLEX. This type of class is usually taught in grades 6 through 9 and lasts from 4 to 12 weeks. FLEX classes are designed to give students an introduction to one or more foreign languages and their cultures. Does this scenario apply to you? If so, then welcome to *¡Buen viaje!: Learning About Our Spanish-Speaking Friends* around the World.

There are those who complain that the exploratory course misleads students because it appears to be "all fun and games". Comments like this only serve to perpetuate the myth that learning a second language must be painful to be valuable. Some teachers voice the regret that they cannot teach enough to "prepare" students for further language study. However, the only preparation necessary for an exploratory experience is one of a positive attitude toward learning language and the predisposition to engage in further language study.

As you begin this journey into the discovery of another language and culture with your students, let's look at the purposes of the exploratory language class. The goals are modest. The expectations are reasonable:

> *To Create a Positive Attitude Toward
> Language Learning,
> the Language Being Explored,
> and Other People and Cultures.*

Some common goals of a FLEX class are to:

- create an awareness of language as a vehicle for communication,

- introduce the functional purpose of language study,

- present the sound systems of another language,

- present functional vocabulary, phrases, and even grammar of another language,

- instill an appreciation of other people and cultures, and

- provide motivation to continue learning another language.

Second language acquisition is not the only goal of an exploratory class because learning a second language is a skill-acquiring and skill-using process that takes place over an extended period of time. A FLEX class does not usually provide the necessary time to consider second language acquisition as a primary goal. If, on the other hand, a longer time sequence is available, then more attention should be given to language acquisition.

You probably have students representing a wide range of learning styles and linguistic abilities. That's why the authors of *¡Buen viaje!* have designed materials to give you a variety of options in your teaching. The materials are intended to be utilized in the manner best suited to you, the teacher, and your students.

Approach your exploratory class with pride and enthusiasm! For most students this will be their first experience with another language. For some, it will be their only one. Make it positive, worthwhile, pleasant, and stimulating! Use all the tools at your disposal! Be creative! Enjoy yourself and your students will enjoy learning about Spanish-speaking friends around the world.

TO THE TEACHER

This instructor's manual is designed to give you general background information as well as specific suggestions that will help you use the material included in *¡Buen viaje!*. It contains information for the language specialist as well as for those of you who may have only limited experience with a second language. You will be well served to take time (and we know your time is at a premium!) to review these materials prior to teaching your course and to refer to this information periodically while the course is in progress.

THE ADOLESCENT/PRE-ADOLESCENT LEARNER

As a teacher in the middle level grades, you work with a very special learner. Here are a few reminders to help you as you teach your exploratory language class.

There are many characteristics typical of the middle level learner. Young adolescents are largely concrete, not abstract learners and have an average attention span of 11.5 minutes. They are growing faster than at any time except for the first year of life. They are physically uncomfortable after sitting 20–25 minutes. As middle level teachers, we have to consider not only our students' cognitive styles and abilities, but all of their physical, social, and emotional characteristics as well.

The growth spurt happens first to early adolescent females. This spurt is over for both the females and males by late adolescence. Many of the changes related to physiology and physical structure create issues that are also reflected in social and emotional characteristics. Your students may exhibit extreme fluctuation in their energy levels. This is probably due to poor eating and sleeping habits, which are common among this age group. It is not unusual for students to need more sleep than they actually get because of the extreme physical changes. Their physical "growing pains" are real! If no legitimate outlet is provided in the class, students will find ways to move around. Thus, you should involve the students physically through activities such as total physical response (TPR), role-play, skits, learning centers, projects, and games.

The social characteristics of the middle level learner are usually much more obvious to the teacher. "Playing around" and "acting up" become predominant in early to middle adolescence. Risk taking, which begins to be exhibited at this time can continue for several years. Adolescents are usually more open minded and willing to explore. This can work to your advantage as you encourage your students to explore the language and culture of other countries.

It is crucial to remember that peer pressure is very strong at this time, and students are fearful of exposing themselves to the disapproval of their peers. This emphasizes the importance of pair and small group work in the language classroom. Even though they may be risk takers, conformity becomes a real issue, and middle level students are especially sensitive when being singled out or made to feel conspicuous in front of an entire class.

Young adolescents tend to think that everything and everyone is focused on them and their appearance, a phenomenon referred to as the "imaginary audience". They rely on their peers for support. Small group, cooperative, and pair learning experiences provide a safe, informal, and comfortable learning environment. This kind of structure will also promote the development of socialization skills and positive interdependence. These activities also promote face-to-face communication. Since the purpose of language is communication, the more communicative the focus of the classroom activities, the more language learning will be made possible!

Emotionally, middle level students are extremely fragile. They may internalize their emotional hurting. Depression and alienation are common in this age group. Again, pair and small group activities in the classroom provide a safer arena for interdependence and tolerance.

The attention span of middle level students may vary greatly. The exploratory class will be much more successful if the teacher is flexible. Plan varied and purposeful activities that take into account the varied attention spans and energy levels. Be ready to change the pace or shift to a different activity!

Remember, middle level students are still largely concrete learners! Grammar and its abstract concepts are difficult if not impossible for many adolescents. The materials in *¡Buen viaje!* are designed for an active hands-on approach to learning. Use concrete objects whenever possible. Visuals, props, and realia all help to facilitate comprehension and communication. Anything that can be touched, smelled, and felt will get students involved in multi-sensory activities. Students like to cut, paste, color, and draw! The good news is that these so-called "fun" activities actually promote language acquisition.

Finally, adolescents are much more motivated by short-term goals. Career options, college opportunities, and the intrinsic value of learning another language mean little to them. Help them see the relevance of language to their own lives by giving them meaningful opportunities to use the language in real life situations. This is the reason why the *¡Buen viaje!* materials are designed around a possible student visit to another country. In many cases, this opportunity is available to them. Even if the real life opportunity doesn't exist, the possibility of imagining the event through role play and other related activities makes the entire concept more "real". As you consider their focus on the "now", remember to help your students by giving them well defined and meaningful tasks. Open-ended and long range projects may cause difficulty and result in their feeling overwhelmed.

The unique characteristics of the middle level learner are, in many ways, an ideal match to the unique characteristics of a FLEX class. Students are offered an opportunity to explore and have fun without the pressure of learning a given body of knowledge. Language learning is a process that takes place over an extended time period. The materials in this book offer your students the opportunity to begin that process. We certainly hope it will be a *¡Buen viaje!*

BUILDING LANGUAGE SKILLS IN THE FLEX CLASSROOM

The purpose of language is communication. Even within the time constraints of the FLEX class, students can begin to explore the acquisition of a second language. Make your classroom a place where the climate is low in anxiety and high in student interest. Integrate the skills of listening, speaking, reading, and writing in a holistic approach to language learning.

The thematic approach used in the *¡Buen viaje!* program is in keeping with a holistic approach to language learning that is sometimes referred to as "whole language." There has been much discussion regarding a precise definition of whole language. Close examination sees it as good teaching characterized in part by thematic lessons, process writing, and interdisciplinary studies.

Second language teachers recognize the "whole language approach" as good sound teaching techniques and strategies that have been in place in the second language classroom for a number of years. These techniques and strategies exist because language teachers review assumptions about teaching and learning. They are researchers in their own classrooms. Their strategies are developed and refined based on what they see and know is working in their classrooms as well as what they read in current research and literature.

Assume that your students can and will learn the material presented in your lessons. Make your classroom a student-centered classroom. Avoid the urge to "impart information" to the learners. Students will learn material when they perceive it to be interesting and meaningful to them.

These materials offer students the opportunity to use all of the four language skills of listening, speaking, reading, and writing, at a level that is reasonable for a FLEX class. The four language skills develop in a progressive manner in primary language acquisition. Research also tells us that oral and written language may be acquired simultaneously in a second language.

Since your students already know one language, they possess a "data bank" from which they are able to draw information and make inferences regarding this experience with a second language. At this very basic FLEX experience level, functional reading and writing as well as speaking and listening should be integral parts of this classroom experience.

Nevertheless, at this level, allow ample time for language input before you expect output. Much of the emphasis in your lessons should be on listening and speaking. Listening provides the platform on which the remaining skills are built. What students hear is their initiation into the language. Total Physical Response (TPR) activities promote active listening. Students may respond by a physical movement to a command or they may pantomime actions as the teacher describes them. Linking together several of these short statements creates a "story line" for the students to follow and adds meaningful context to the words. Contextualizing language through visuals, realia, and props also helps students understand what is being said.

Students should not be expected to respond orally if they do not feel ready to do so. Initially, it may be helpful to teach some classroom phrases or words, which students can use on a daily basis. These "passwords", using the target language, can make learners comfortable and instill a sense of confidence in their ability to use the language in a meaningful manner. Be sure to model the words and phrases with natural speed and intonation. It is always better to rely on more repetition than to slow down or exaggerate pronunciation. This only distorts the language. Avoid teaching pronunciation for the sake of pronunciation. This causes students to focus on the mechanics rather than the meaning of the message.

The active skills of speaking and writing, lag behind the passive skills of listening and reading. Reading and writing in a FLEX class are minimal and carefully controlled. Making lists and copying words and phrases are considered writing activities. Reading what has been copied or written is a legitimate reading activity. The ability to read and write in the target language will be closely tied to the ability to speak.

The key to leading students to even minimal second language acquisition is to present the material in a context that is communicative and meaningful to the learner. Encourage your students and give them opportunities to communicate with one another through pair and small group activities. The activities in the individual Elements are designed for this kind of meaningful communicative interaction.

BUILDING CULTURAL AWARENESS IN THE FLEX CLASSROOM

Our world is becoming more globally interdependent. Our students must, therefore, become more culturally sensitive as well as more linguistically proficient. One of the major goals of a FLEX class is to instill an appreciation of other people and cultures. The *¡Buen viaje!* program offers numerous activities with which you can heighten student cultural awareness. A multicultural approach is one that sees the oneness and sameness of people throughout the world. Encourage your students to recognize their own cultural identity and heritage. A cultural self-awareness leads to a receptive state of mind with respect to diversity.

Work with other teachers in your school to develop lessons and projects that are interdisciplinary and have multicultural themes. Not only will this help students develop their multicultural awareness, but it will help everyone involved to see second language study as an integral and interrelated part of the total school curriculum. Music, Art, Literature, Science, Mathematics, and Social Studies can all be linked to other cultures. Where it is especially appropriate, you will find specific **interdisciplinary** suggestions on the opening page of each Element in the Teacher's Manual.

Language and culture are so intricately interwoven that it has been said that the only way to truly know and understand a people is by learning their language. Although knowledge of their language is an indispensable asset to understanding other people, it is not in and of itself a guarantee. A similar knowledge of the social attitudes must also exist. Many of the suggested activities in this material will require students to seek information from a library, computer data base, and/or individuals. Try to use and/or develop activities that encourage interaction with ethnic groups and their members in your own community as an excellent start toward developing multicultural awareness.

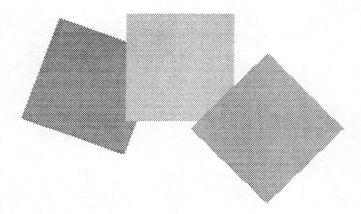

TEACHING STRATEGIES FOR THE FLEX CLASSROOM

Cooperative Learning

The major principles of cooperative learning strategies are invaluable as a teaching tool in a FLEX classroom. These principles help to define the roles of teachers and students in class, and to incorporate student learning styles. They are based on the idea that students can learn as much from each other as they can from the teacher as long as they do so in a spirit of cooperation. The following principles are central to cooperative learning:

- Teaching must be student centered.

- Paired and small-group work is essential to engage students in frequent communication that is meaningful, based on real-world experiences, relatively free of anxiety, and challenging to various learning styles and abilities.

- Cooperative learning encourages multiple forms of expression.

- It promotes positive interdependence and creates a positive social atmosphere in which students learn to accept the contributions that others can make to their learning.

- It fosters the willingness to be helpful to others through shared responsibility.

- It promotes individual expression of likes, dislikes, and preferences rather than "cloned" behavior.

- It allows students to manipulate language in ways that are most suitable to them.

- It gives teachers the opportunity to relax and be the observers of student behavior, thus enhancing sensitivity to student needs and abilities.

Total Physical Response (TPR)

The Total Physical Response Approach to teaching is based on several theories that indicate how individuals can learn a foreign language quickly and still have long-term retention. The theories are based on studies of first-language acquisition, and TPR is a condensed simulation of how children learn.

Assumptions:

- It is easier to learn a foreign language in a stress-free environment.

- Learning a foreign language should be enjoyable.

- With children, listening precedes speaking: i.e., they spend thousands of hours listening to the language before they are able to utter coherent words.

- Children associate words with actions: i.e., the movement of their entire bodies.

- Language and actions are often transmitted to children through commands.

- Children speak when they are ready to speak. They are not forced to do so.

Many classroom studies with children and adults have demonstrated that TPR is an effective way to teach a foreign language, particularly during the early stages of language acquisition. The approach lends itself perfectly to a FLEX classroom.

UTILIZING TECHNOLOGY IN THE FOREIGN LANGUAGE CLASSROOM

Foreign language teaching is undergoing a dramatic change in the 1990's. Today's foreign language classroom focuses increasingly on communication. Teachers are striving to provide multiple opportunities for students to use their newly acquired language skills in real life situations. These opportunities will prepare them to participate fully in a multilingual international community.

This functional orientation to language teaching and learning can be enhanced and supported by the use of technology. Using technology in the foreign language classroom has expanded from the limits of simple language labs, tape recorders, and video tapes to a plethora of new opportunities, many of which integrate a variety of technologies. Computer programs are integrated with CD-ROM and video-disc. Multimedia packages further integrate computers, video, CD-ROM, and video-disc. Today's language labs include interactive video, networked computers, and multimedia capabilities. Satellite broadcasts offer distance learning options connecting language classes not only within a school district, but also among cities, states, countries, and continents.

As teachers shift from being disseminators of information to facilitators of learning, the use of technology offers students a broader range of opportunities in which to use new language skills. E-Mail and electronic bulletin boards can link the rich assets of bilingual communities with students of the language of that community, thus providing linguistic and cultural interaction. By using CD-ROM and distance learning, teachers are able to integrate content area instruction in the language classroom supported by real life materials in the target language.

As we incorporate technology into the teaching and learning of the foreign language classroom, we bring additional cultures and languages to our doorstep. The use of technology expands and enhances the opportunities offered to language students and enables them to become fully functioning citizens of the new century.

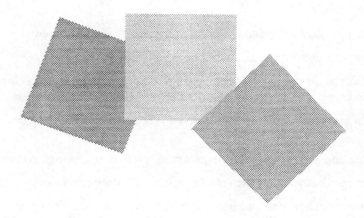

ASSESSMENT AND EVALUATION

Any discussion of assessment, evaluation, and testing is closely tied to considerations of grading. In some FLEX classes teachers are not required to give formal letter grades. It is desirable, however, to assess the progress of students in a FLEX classroom. Learners need to be given a sense of accomplishment. Therefore, any evaluation in the class should focus on what the students know and can do. Evaluation should not be designed to show what the students may not have learned.

Students perform best when their anxiety level is low. In a FLEX class, using grades, particularly those based on paper and pencil tests, is counter-productive to sound instructional strategies. Particularly at a period in their lives when they are struggling with their own identity, adolescent learners need a sense of self-worth based, in part, on their accomplishments. If you are required to give tests and grades, incorporate the suggestions given here. Give credit for the efforts students expend and reward even the slightest progress through your praise and encouragement.

Formal paper and pencil tests are inappropriate for a FLEX class. You are encouraged to seek alternative ways of evaluating student progress. The materials presented in ¡Buen viaje! are formatted to encourage students to use higher order thinking skills. Many of the activities may also be used as a means of evaluation. Remember to test what has been taught in the same way in which it was taught. The focus of these teaching materials is one of communication. Use these same kinds of communicative activities for evaluation. The end of each Element has a Journal Page for the students to summarize their learning. This page is an excellent means of summarizing, reviewing, and evaluating what they have learned.

Much of what your students will be doing relies on listening and speaking. They will understand more than they are able to say. The skill of listening is a receptive skill and develops first. You may evaluate *listening* by giving commands and having the students perform those commands to show their understanding. Showing pictures and making statements that require only a true-false response also enables you to check listening comprehension.

Your students will be developing their oral language skills by engaging in activities that are communicative and contextualized. When you evaluate their *speaking* skills, the function should be the same. You might ask them to talk about a picture, answer a familiar question, or simply give an appropriate oral response to a statement.

Reading and *writing* skills will be much less developed within the parameters of a FLEX class. Look at the many activities provided in ¡Buen viaje! and select some that can be used for evaluation purposes. Matching labels with pictures is a way of testing their ability to read. A parallel activity will evaluate writing if you require the students to write rather than match the labels.

It is imperative to test material in the same way in which it was taught. It is also important to remember the progression to the higher order thinking skills. Literal simple recall requires much less of the learner than having to react critically and creatively. The following strategies proceed from the simpler to the more complex. They are listed to guide you in evaluation, but they are also to be considered as options for daily instruction.

Strategies for Evaluation and Instruction

Literal evaluation strategies require students to recall or recognize information by:

listening	naming
telling	identifying
defining	labeling

Interpretive evaluation strategies require students to demonstrate their understanding of the material by:

explaining	describing
discussing	classifying
contrasting	comparing

Critical evaluation strategies require students to demonstrate that they can solve problems, separate information, and make judgements by:

dramatizing	judging	illustrating
evaluating	applying	measuring
expanding	deciding	analyzing
distinguishing	experimenting	predicting

Creative evaluation strategies require students to solve a problem by putting information together that requires original, creative thinking by:

combining	constructing
inventing	designing

Consistent and systematic evaluation and assessment will benefit the learner in a FLEX class. Achievement testing gives students a chance to show what they have learned. When this type of assessment takes place in a secure, supportive, and low anxiety environment, students gain confidence and increase their opportunities for further learning.

HOW TO USE THE ELEMENTS: AN OVERVIEW

All of the materials in *¡Buen viaje!* are organized around the central theme of planning for and going to visit another country where the language is spoken. There are two main sections: Predeparture and Homestay. Within each section there are six "Elements of Discovery", or lessons, from which you can select those that are appropriate and of interest to you and your students. The final Element in each section (Numbers 7 and 13) is designed to review the material covered in the preceding six lessons. It is not necessary to use the entire book sequentially. *¡Buen viaje!* was developed to accommodate a variety of exploratory language course curricular designs and goals. The authors realize that exploratory language courses vary in length and depth of instruction.

Each Element has a theme. The themes represent activities that might be associated with predeparture planning for the trip, or with events after the student arrives in his or her selected homestay country. Individual Elements are similar in length. You may want to take several class periods to cover each Element, depending on the length of the class period and the number of weeks the class meets. Add your own favorite activities or develop others that relate to the theme of the Element. We suggest that you brainstorm some thematic webbing with your class to extend the activities beyond those presented in the book. Learning takes place best when the students see it as relevant to themselves. Use their interests and ideas to build on what is presented in the book.

LEARNING ABOUT HOMESTAY COUNTRIES, CITIES, AND LANGUAGES

Picture card #1 "Youth conference" may be used with this element.

Contents

1. **Communicative Functions:**

   Socializing, exchanging information, expressing and finding out attitudes

2. **Content and Language Skills:**

   Buenos días, Me llamo, Soy de, Mucho gusto, geography of Hispanic countries and cities, cognates

3. **Culture:**

   Cultural awareness and sensitivity, increasing self-awareness, comparing cultures

4. **Teaching and Learning Strategies:**

   Playing games, doing puzzles, researching, developing geography skills, webbing thematically

Additional Activity Suggestions (Extension and Interdisciplinary)

1. **Social Studies**

   - Invite exchange students and/or guest speakers from student exchange programs to class.
   - Hold a model U.N. meeting.
   - Hold a mock international youth conference.
   - Plan field trips to local ethnic clubs, churches, or an international institute.
   - Practice using maps and globes.
   - Do projects using computer data bases.

2. **Mathematics**

   - Analyze local, state, or federal census data regarding ethnicity.

3. **Language Arts**

   - Plan a lesson about language families.
   - Have students do written and/or oral reports about Hispanic influences in their community and state.

4. **Advisor/Advisee or Homeroom**

   - Hold discussions with students about their attitudes toward other cultures.

Special Notes to the Teacher

In these materials you will see the use of three terms: *variation, expansion,* and *extension*. *Variation* activities are directly related to the information being presented and offer a slightly different perspective and/or option for presentation and/or practice. *Expansion* notes are also related directly to the information being presented and are intended to expand the material. *Extension* materials are those such as interdisciplinary activities that may be only tangentially related to the original material. Extension activities are a "spin-off" from the original and are intended to offer a variety of activities, including some which may not have language acquisition as a goal.

Things to Remember About Language Learning

Encourage students to guess the meanings of new words either as cognates (this concept is introduced in this Element) or from context. They should use this same approach throughout the text. Emphasize the value of looking at context, pictures, and illustrations for clues to meaning. Learning a new language is a risk-taking adventure. Tell students that they are embarking on a real-life "treasure hunt." The prize will be their ability to communicate, even a little, with speakers of Spanish. Many students are intrigued by the notion of being able to use words and phrases as a "code." Appeal to their imagination as well as to their sense of fun and adventure.

You may want to discuss briefly the fact that Spanish is a phonetic language and that this can help students with pronunciation. Resist the urge to overcorrect pronunciation and structure. Opt instead for a relaxed approach in which students are encouraged to have fun and experiment with the language.

In later Elements you will find the use of *interlanguage* (the mixing of English and Spanish) as a natural way to encourage second language development. Some activity direction lines will also give students the opportunity to use *subvocalization* (whispering to oneself) as a building block to second language acquisition.

PERSPECTIVA

The **Perspectiva** is an advance organizer intended to stimulate discussion about the topic to be covered in this Element. Ask students to look at the map and think about the Element's theme—Spanish-speaking countries and the Spanish language. If any of the students are of Hispanic background, and they feel comfortable discussing this, ask them to talk about their family and the area from which they came. It is important to validate the differences and similarities in ethnic background and heritage. Keep in mind that middle-level students are extremely sensitive about their self-image.

As you introduce this Element, also present the overall theme of the homestay. Students should be thinking in terms of selecting a country for their imaginary homestay. If you have any exchange students in your school or district, arrange to have them come and talk to the class about their exchange experience. There are many organizations that plan exchange visits. Encourage students to contact those organizations and/or individuals who may be able to give them background and information.

VARIATION

BLM 1.0. Make a transparency of the Blackline master **BLM 1.0**. Using the transparency, help students focus on the topics to be covered in this Element. This transparency may also be used as a culminating and/or assessment activity.

Finally, this is your chance to set the tone for the class experience. Be positive, enthusiastic, and enjoy!

A. INTERNATIONAL YOUTH CONFERENCE

Introduce the Spanish words **muchachos** *(boys)*, **muchachas** *(girls)*, and **país** *(country)*. Ask students if they are familiar with these words. Go over the list of names and countries in Spanish. If students would like to do so, allow them to select a Spanish name for themselves. Let them see whether there is an equivalent to their English name in Spanish. Sometimes students like to select an entirely different name, even if their name has a Spanish equivalent.

VARIATION

BLM 1.0. Using a transparency of the map of the Spanish-speaking world, help students locate the countries associated with each name.

B. MEETING NEW FRIENDS

Read the name tags with students.

Answer Key:

1. Buenos días

2. *My name is*

3. Soy de

4. Eduardo, María Luisa, Miguel

5. María Luisa

6. Eduardo, Miguel

7. España, Nicaragua, Argentina

8. España is in Europe, Nicaragua is in Central America, and Argentina is in South America.

9. María Luisa

EXPANSION

Meeting New Friends Bingo. (BLM 1.1 and 1.2) Duplicate enough copies of the bingo sheets for the entire class. Introduce the expression **Mucho gusto** and explain its use as equivalent to the English *I'm pleased to meet you.* You may wish to explain that boys should say **Encantado** and girls say **Encantada**. The concept of gender agreement is formally presented in Element 2.

Version One: Directions to Students

You are now going to use your four new Spanish expressions, **Buenos días, Me llamo, Soy de,** and **Mucho gusto,** to meet and greet new Spanish-speaking friends.

1. Choose a name from the conference list and make your own name tag.

2. Find out the names chosen by your classmates.

3. Choose 16 names and write one name randomly in each block of the grid.

4. Go around the room and greet each person by name, saying **Buenos días, (Roberto). Me llamo (Ana María)**. The person being greeted responds by saying **Mucho gusto** (or **Encantado/a** if it has been taught). Then that person initials the block with the other person's name in it. When a student has four in a row, he or she wins. (You may decide to see who can get all of the blocks first.)

Version Two: Directions to Students

1. Choose a name from the conference list and make your own name tag. Be sure to fill in your country name.

2. Find out the names chosen by your classmates.

3. Choose 16 different Spanish-speaking countries from the conference list and write the name of one country randomly in each block.

4. Go around the room and greet each person by name, saying **Buenos días, (Roberto). Me llamo (Ana María)**. The person being greeted responds by saying **Mucho gusto** (or **Encantado/a** if it has been taught). Then that person initials the block with the name of the other person's country in it. When a student has four in a row, he or she wins. (You may decide to see who can get all of the blocks first.)

Version Three: Directions to Teacher

1. Choose 16 Spanish-speaking countries.

2. Cut small pieces of paper, one for each student.

3. Write a different Spanish-speaking country on each piece of paper. (If you have more than 16 students in class, then reuse several countries.)

4. Have students fill out the bingo board with the names of the 16 countries in random positions.

5. Distribute a piece of paper with the name of a country to each student. Instruct students to keep their country a secret.

6. Instruct students to go around the room and greet each person by saying **Buenos días, (Roberto). Me llamo (Ana María)**. The person being greeted responds by saying **Mucho gusto** (or **Encantado/a** if that has been taught). Then that person initials the block with the name of the other person's country in it. When a student has four in a row, he or she wins. (You may decide to see who can get all of the blocks first.)

C. YOUTH AMBASSADOR

Begin this activity with a discussion of what it means to be an "ambassador." Have a student(s) look up the meaning of the word in the dictionary.

1. Individual

Encourage students to spend some time thinking about their own lives and the kinds of positive things they would like other people to know about them and life in the United States. It is important to get students to focus on the positive aspects of their lives. This may be difficult in some cases, especially if students come from a socially or economically deprived background. If the reality of their existence is not positive, encourage them to visualize and imagine what they would like it to become. Use that image as the basis for their sharing.

2. Group

Have students share their ideas with a small group of classmates, including what they will tell their host families about these things. When they have all listened to each other, give them time to write new ideas in their own suitcase if they wish.

EXPANSION

Youth Ambassador Class Project. (BLM 1.3)

1. While students are in their groups, have one serve as recorder for the group. Hand a copy of the Blackline Master to each group. Any response that all members of the group can reach consensus on for their group should be added to this copy of the Youth Ambassador suitcase.

2. Report group responses to the class and develop a class consensus, possibly using an overhead transparency made from the Blackline Master. This will serve as a generalization for the teens in your area.

D. SPAIN

Answer Key:

A. 1. Océano Atlántico

  2. Mar Mediterráneo

  3. Estrecho de Gibraltar

B. 1. Pirineos, Sierra Nevada, Sierra de Guadarrama

  2. Río Guadalquivir

  3. Río Tajo

  4. Río Ebro

  5. Two; answers may include the following: swim, water-ski, jet ski, sail, sunbathe

  6. Teacher must check student responses: Madrid, Toledo, Río Tajo, Estrecho de Gibraltar, etc.

EXPANSION

Spain Jigsaw Puzzle. (BLM 1.4 and 1.5) Distribute one copy per student of both 1.4 and 1.5. Go over instructions with students before they begin.

E. CITIES IN SPAIN

Review the names of the cities with students. Students then complete the activity as directed in their book. This activity can easily be expanded in a number of ways by allowing students to do reports or another investigative activity about cities. For example, what is the origin of the name of the city? Why was the city founded? Is the city located on or near a major river or body of water and, if so, why?

EXPANSION

Find the three largest cities in Spain. Compare them with the three largest cities in the United States (or in your state) with regard to geographic location (longitude/latitude), population, and date founded.

F. MEXICO, CENTRAL AMERICA, AND THE CARIBBEAN

Tell students to look carefully at the map of Mexico and Central America and also to refer to the map of the Spanish-speaking world. Go over the terms in Spanish.

Answer Key:

A. 1. Océano Pacífico

2. Océano Atlántico

3. Golfo de México

4. Mar Caribe

B. 1. Sierra Madre—Sierra Madre Occidental, Sierra Madre Oriental, Sierra Madre del Sur

2. Canal de Panamá

3. Cuba

4. Baja California

5. Península de Yucatán

6. Sierra Madre

7. Guatemala, Honduras, El Salvador, Nicaragua, Costa Rica, Panamá

8. México

9. Río Grande

10. Teacher must check student responses: Península de Yucatán, Canal de Panamá, Costa Rica, etc.

EXPANSION

Mexico, Central America, and the Caribbean Jigsaw Puzzle. (BLM 1.6 and 1.7) Distribute one copy per student of both 1.6 and 1.7. Go over instructions with students before they begin.

G. SOUTH AMERICA

Tell students to look carefully at the map of South America. Review the terms in Spanish.

Answer Key:

A. 1. Océano Pacífico

2. Océano Atlántico

3. Golfo de México

4. Mar Caribe

B. 1. Cordillera de los Andes

2. Río Orinoco

3. Río Amazonas

4. Río Amazonas, Río Orinoco

5. Bolivia, Paraguay

6. Los Andes / Venezuela, Colombia, Ecuador, Perú, Bolivia, Argentina, Chile

7. July: Colombia, Venezuela, Ecuador, Perú / December: Argentina, Uruguay, Chile

8. Teacher must check student responses: Los Andes, Río Amazonas, etc.

EXPANSION

South America Jigsaw Puzzle. (BLM 1.8 and 1.9) Distribute one copy per student of both 1.8 and 1.9. Go over instructions with students before they begin.

H. RECOGNIZING COUNTRIES AND CONTINENTS

Answer Key:

1.	S	7.	A
2.	E	8.	S
3.	S	9.	N
4.	S	10.	S
5.	N	11.	S
6.	S	12.	S

EXPANSION

To review the country locations with students, place country names on 3 X 5 index cards. In pairs or small groups, have students sort countries by continent. Have students draw maps after the countries are sorted. This is a culminating activity that can be used for partial assessment of geographic information.

EXPANSION

Country Research Activity. (BLM 1.10) Give each student a copy of the Country Research Form. Go over the directions and assist students in deciding where they might find the information they need.

EXPANSION

City Research Activity. (BLM 1.11) Follow the same procedure as for the Country Research Activity.

I. SPANISH WORDS YOU KNOW: COGNATES

Discuss the concept of cognates with students. Review the list together, discussing meanings. The indicated genders may be ignored at this point. If you choose to ignore them, you can tell students that **el** and **la** are explained in Element 2. You may want, at least, to say that both words mean *the*.

EXPANSION

Word Collage. Have students make a cognate collage using pictures they cut out from magazines and catalogues. Supply these materials or have students bring them to class. Directions to students:

1. Choose 15 words from the cognate list.

2. Find a picture in a magazine that represents each word.

3. Cut out the pictures and glue them artistically on construction paper, leaving a half-inch space around the edges in which to write.

4. Write the words near the pictures around the edges, carefully copying them from the list.

VARIATION

Students who are artistically inclined should be encouraged to draw the pictures.

EXPANSION

Make Your Own Word Bank. To organize this project, have each student bring in a 3 × 5 file box or a shoebox and a package of 3 × 5 index cards. When these files are made, they can be used in individual, pair, or group activities.

Directions to students:

1. Use a shoebox or recipe holder as your container.

2. Write words to be remembered on a file card.

3. Cut out a picture or draw one representing the word.

4. Put the picture or some other cue on the reverse side of the card.

5. If you have divider cards, you can group your word cards alphabetically, thematically, etc., in your box.

6. You can use your word bank to:

   • review vocabulary

   • form thematic categories

   • practice alphabetizing with the Spanish alphabet

   • practice matching of opposites, feminine/masculine, verbs, etc.

   You may also use them as:

   • a dictionary

   • a basis for writing projects/short dialogues

   • bingo words

   • Jeopardy answers

J. COGNATE CATEGORIES

Have students complete the webbing activity according to the directions.
Culminating Activity: Review the entire Element with students. Encourage them to think of other thematic webs that relate to the vocabulary from this Element (example: Mountains/Rivers).

K. MY JOURNAL

Explain to students that the journal entry is going to be their way of summarizing the material they have covered in each Element. Introduce the terms **Mis palabras** (*My words*), **Información nueva** (*New information*), and **Mi dibujo** (*My drawing*). Encourage as much use of the Spanish language as possible. Do not be overly concerned with accuracy. This is an entry-level experience, and its goal is to encourage and facilitate second language acquisition. Using interlanguage (mixing English and Spanish) helps the learner move into fuller use of the target language.

If you are going to use this as an assessment tool, be very clear about your expectations with regard to content and accuracy. It is imperative to use the same mode for assessment as instruction. Do not teach one way and assess another. The material in *¡Buen viaje!* is designed to develop only minimal skill in second language acquisition. The focus is on exploration of, and motivation to, study another language. Assessment should be authentic and ongoing. It should be used for the purpose of assisting students with their language development, not for grades. If you must give grades in your classes, you are encouraged to consider all aspects of students' behavior in the classroom, i.e., participation, cooperation, and willingness to learn.

2 PACKING

Picture cards 2a "Clothing store" and 2b "Girl in bedroom packing" are designed for use with this element but many of the other cards can also be used for identifying colors and articles of clothing.

Contents

1. **Communicative Functions:**

   Identifying, reporting (describing), exchanging information, inquiring, reading, expressing preference

2. **Content and Language Skills:**

   Common articles of clothing, basic colors, cardinal numbers 1–10, gender and number (masculine/feminine, singular/plural), definite articles (**el, la, los, las**), indefinite articles (**un, una**), adjective agreement with colors

3, **Culture:**

   Differences in calendars and using numbers.

4. **Teaching and Learning Strategies:**

   Listening selectively, grouping, doing puzzles, playing games, using Total Physical Response (TPR), role playing

Additional Activity Suggestions (Extension and Interdisciplinary)

1. **Social Studies**
   - Discuss similarities and differences in clothing based on where people live in the world.

2. **Mathematics**
   - Discuss the difference between cardinal and ordinal numbers.

3. **Science**
   - Invite the science faculty to teach a lesson on what causes color and on how a color prism works.
   - Have students do research on how numbers are used in astrology and astronomy.

4. **Art**
   - Have students create posters or collages using colors and clothing.
   - Discuss the use of color by famous Spanish artists (schools).

5. **Advisor/Advisee or Homeroom**
   - Hold discussions about peer influence on dress and whether there should be a school dress code or uniform.

Special Notes to the Teacher

In these materials you will see the use of three terms: variation, expansion, and extension. *Variation* activities are directly related to the information being presented and offer a slightly different perspective and/or option for presentation and/or practice. *Expansion* notes are also related directly to the information being presented and are intended to expand the material. *Extension* materials are those such as interdisciplinary activities that may be only tangentially related to the original material. Extension activities are a "spin-off" from the original and are intended to offer a variety of activities, including some which may not have language acquisition as a goal.

In this Element you will also begin to see, in the student book, a small drawing of a post-it note labeled **NOTA.** This visual cue indicates a note containing special information about language or culture. Alert students to watch for these special hints.

Things to Remember About Language Learning

If you have not already done so, you may want to discuss briefly the fact that Spanish is a phonetic language and that this can help students with pronunciation. Remind students about cognates and how these words can also be helpful to their understanding of the language. Encourage guessing and risk taking as this Element introduces more language. Resist the urge to overcorrect pronunciation and structure. Opt instead for a relaxed approach in which students are encouraged to have fun and experiment with the language.

In this Element you will find more use of *interlanguage* (the mixing of English and Spanish) as a natural way to encourage second language development. Some activity direction lines will also give students the opportunity to use *subvocalization* (whispering to oneself) as a building block to second language acquisition.

PERSPECTIVA

The **Perspectiva** is an advance organizer intended to stimulate discussion about the topics to be covered in this Element. Ask students to look at the picture. Discuss items that are shown. Elicit responses that indicate items of clothing, colors, and numbers. Direct their attention to the upside-down question mark. Show them how Spanish uses this at the beginning of a question, as well as at the beginning of an exclamation.

VARIATION

Perspectiva. (BLM 2.0) Make a transparency of BLM 2.0. Use it to help students focus on the topics to be covered in this Element. This transparency may also be used as a culminating and/or assessment activity.

A. CLOTHING

This activity has two purposes: 1) to introduce names of some common articles of clothing and other personal items students would be likely to take for a homestay, and 2) to present the definite articles el, la, los, and las. (Las is only presented in the activity. Students do not use it in the webbing exercise.) Abstract grammatical concepts are difficult for the transescent learner. Keep any and all discussion of grammar to a minimum. Never present grammar unless it is within the context of the material students are using in the lesson.

If at all possible, have the actual clothing/travel items in the classroom. Several days before presenting this Element, put a list on the board of the items you will need. Students sign up to bring in items. You may want more than one of each item to facilitate introduction of numbers and colors.

As you introduce the clothing and other items, briefly explain that you will be using one of the Spanish words for *the* along with the name of the item. Students will not need to "translate" the definite article, but should be encouraged to learn the article along with the noun. Explain that later they will need to know the correct Spanish form of *the* when using other descriptors.

Use a lot of movement and gestures as you present the vocabulary. It will be easier if you present the new word by showing the item and saying (for example), **Tengo la blusa.** Then repeat, **la blusa,** and show the item. Repeat this for each item. Move around the room and allow students to see and touch the item. When students seem relatively comfortable with the vocabulary, have them proceed to the webbing activity.

EXPANSION

After presenting the 21 items, use TPR to practice with students. Use actual items or pictures. Have students stand in a circle. Walk behind them and give each one an item (actual/replica/picture), telling them to keep their article hidden behind their back. Then step to the center of the circle and ask each student, **¿Qué tienes?** The student should answer, **Tengo _____.** Continue until each student has spoken. If your class is too large, do one half at a time. Students who are observing can be asked to keep track on a sheet of paper by writing the name of the student and the article he or she has. If there are more than 21 students, give out duplicates of a few items.

EXPANSION

Before beginning this activity, teach the Spanish word **y** *(and)* to help students link the vocabulary together. Ask students to stand in a circle, giving each one an item. Tell the first student to begin by saying **Tengo,** followed by the name of the item (e.g., **Tengo una camiseta).** Ask the student to hand that item to the next student, who says he or she is holding the first student's item and his or her own (e.g., **Tengo una camiseta y un par de calcetines).** This continues until a student cannot name all of the items. That student is "out" and gives his or her item to the previous student, who must then name all of the items. This continues until one student has all the items and can name them. If the elimination process does not reduce the number to one student, you have multiple winners!

VARIATION

Use the same phrase as above (Tengo _____.) Be sure each student is seated and has an item. The first student randomly walks to another and hands him or her an item. Continue in this fashion until one student has all of the items and can name them.

B. PACKING PRACTICE (BLM 2.1)

This is a TPR activity. Ask students to bring in old magazines and catalogues. If they do not have these at home, encourage them to ask other teachers for these materials. If you prefer, make copies of the Blackline Master of clothing. Extra copies will ensure that students have enough copies of each item of clothing. Put the Spanish names of the items on the board or encourage students to refer to their books or the Blackline Master. Have students cut out items and copy the Spanish name for each on the back. These words may be used to check against, in case the student forgets or needs to review.

Review the steps in the student book. Select five to ten items to begin. Name the items in random order, saying the name of each item twice. Use both the article and the noun; for example, **el vestido.** After going through the list, ask a student volunteer to repeat the articles back to you "bingo style."

VARIATION

Use the overhead projector. With the projector light off, place the cutout forms of the items on the overhead as you dictate them. After naming five to ten items, turn the projector light on. Review names of the items as you remove them from the screen.

VARIATION

Writing/spelling activity. Using the overhead projector and a piece of clear acetate, write the definite article and the name of the item (with the overhead light off) as you dictate them to the class. When finished, turn on the projector light and allow students to check their responses.

C. NUMBERS

HINT: Consult an early elementary teacher or a resource center for games and realia you can use to teach numbers. Materials that are not language specific (such as Cuisinaire rods) are excellent props. Many of these materials use the basic colors and can be utilized in teaching the colors as well.

Introduce the numbers from 1 to 10.

1 uno	3 tres	5 cinco	7 siete	9 nueve
2 dos	4 cuatro	6 seis	8 ocho	10 diez

Be sure students understand the difference between the "numeral" 7 (the arabic digit) and the "number" seven (the word). Use a variety of techniques involving counting to avoid rote memorization of the sequence. Some examples follow:

1. Put the numerals in sequence on the board. Students say or write out the appropriate number as you point to the numerals in random order.

2. Dictate numbers and have students write either the appropriate numeral or the spelled out number on a piece of paper. Verify answers after each number is read. You can also use the overhead projector and uncover each number after you have said it aloud.

3. Have students make 5 × 7 cards using shirt cardboard or pieces of poster board or tag-board. Have them write one numeral on each card, large enough to be seen from the opposite end of the room. Tell them to hold their cards "playing card style" in their hands or to spread them on the desk-

top. As you or a student volunteer says a number in Spanish, students hold up the card showing the corresponding numeral. This can also be done as a timed small-group activity.

D. HOW MANY ARE YOU TAKING?

Read the directions and review the example with students. Then dictate the left column of numbers. Students write the numeral in the first blank. Verify responses by showing the correct numeral on the chalkboard or overhead. When these have all been checked, have students spell out the numbers in the longer blank. Verify spellings.

1.	jeans	2	dos
2.	camisetas	8	ocho
3.	pares de zapatos	5	cinco
4.	pantalones	7	siete
5.	suéter	4	cuatro
6.	vestidos	6	seis
7.	calcetines	9	nueve
8.	faldas	4	cuatro
9.	camisas	10	diez
10.	peinillas	1	uno

Be aware that **uno** is used literally to mean the number *one*. For the indefinite articles *a* or *an* (as in *an umbrella* or *a T-shirt*), **un** or **una** are used (**un paraguas, una camiseta**). This information will be presented in the student book in a later Element. You may want to mention it at this time if it seems developmentally appropriate: **Uno** is for the number alone; **un** and **una** are for use before a noun.

NOTE: Spanish nouns ending in a consonant add -es to form the plural. Singular nouns ending in s, like **paraguas**, use the same form for the plural. **Jeans** and **pantalones** are always plural.

EXPANSION
How Many Are in the Suitcase? (BLM 2.2)

Answer Key:

1.	camisetas	siete
2.	suéteres	seis
3.	chaquetas	dos
4.	pares de zapatos	tres
5.	pares de calcetines	nueve
6.	camisas	ocho
7.	sudaderas	cuatro
8.	jeans	cinco

E. COLORS

Introduce the ten basic colors shown in the student book. Begin by presenting the masculine form of the color. Consult an elementary teacher or a resource store for objects that are not language related and that can be used to teach colors. Use items such as Cuisinaire rods, beads, construction paper, plastic flowers or fruit, and colored crayons or markers. An added cultural component occurs when you use authentic colorful paintings, Mexican sarapes, and rugs or weavings from Latin American countries to teach the colors. Allow ample time for students to practice in pairs or small groups. If you are going to use the book to introduce colors, briefly review counting from 1 to 10. Next, introduce the following colors using the numbered sweaters:

1. rojo *(red)*
2. anaranjado *(orange)*
3. rosado *(pink)*
4. amarillo *(yellow)*
5. azul *(blue)*
6. negro *(black)*
7. verde *(green)*
8. marrón *(brown)*
9. blanco *(white)*
10. violeta *(violet)*

The feminine form of the color (when used as an adjective) will be presented in Activity F. Use the masculine form for purposes of color recognition.

EXPANSION

Use colored toothpicks. Students practice in pairs. They can do simple color identification or practice the numbers 1 to 10 and the colors using TPR. For example, Student A states a number, **dos**, and a color, **rojo**. Student B must give Student A two red toothpicks. Switch roles.

EXPANSION

Laminate sheets of colored construction paper using the colors introduced in Exercise E. (You may introduce additional colors if you wish.) Cut into 2 × 4 strips. Make enough strips for each student to have ten strips of each color. As you call a number and a color, students hold up the appropriate number and color of strips. These can also be used for pairs or small groups.

EXPANSION

Give students paper, crayons, colored markers, and construction paper. Allow them time to draw a picture of anything they'd like. The object is to use all ten colors somewhere in the picture. When the picture is finished, have students label the colors. Display the pictures on a bulletin board.

EXPANSION

Here are the words to the song **"Los colores."** This song is recorded on the Teacher Tape.

Los colores
¡Azul, blanco, rojo, violeta,
amarillo, anaranjado, verde y rosa!
¡Una vez más!
¡Azul, blanco, rojo, violeta,
amarillo, anaranjado, verde y rosa!

From: *Sing, Dance, Laugh, and Eat Tacos!* by Barbara MacArthur
copyright 1990, 6945 Hwy. 14 East, Janesville, WI 53546.

F. THE SUITCASE

Introduce the term **la maleta** for *suitcase*. Remind students again of the Spanish use of el and la before nouns. Then present the concept of adjective agreement using the colors. Do not overemphasize abstract grammatical concepts. Present the idea simply as a "game" or "word match" concept. When used in the plural, all adjectives of color in this activity add **s** except **azules** and **marrones**.

EXPANSION

Camisetas de color. (BLM 2.3) Read the directions with students. Dictate the colors as follows. Since **camiseta** uses **la**, all of the colors will end in **a** except those having only one form (**azul/verde/marrón**). Students fill in the blank with the color. After all blanks are completed, students may color the shirts. Verify the color and its form: 1/**violeta**, 2/**blanca**, 3/**rosada**, 4/**amarilla**, 5/**anaranjada**, 6/**verde**, 7/**azul**, 8/**negra**, 9/**roja**, 10/**marrón**.

Students fill in the blanks following the name of the article in the suitcase compartments. Answers/colors will vary; however, check that the correct form of the color is used. Consult the list in the student book. All items in the EL compartment use the "o" form of the color except for **azul**, **verde**, and **marrón**. All items in the LA compartment use the "a" form of the color except for **azul**, **verde**, and **marrón**. Be sure students use each color at least once.

G. PACKING FOR YOUR TRIP

Read over directions with students. Present the **NOTA**, introducing the plural of the colors.

Answer Key: Item to be circled is in bold print.

1.	jeans azules	red jeans/**blue jeans**/blue slacks
2.	camiseta blanca	white brush/brown T-shirt/**white T-shirt**
3.	chaqueta verde	green skirt/green umbrella/**green jacket**
4.	calcetines blancos	yellow socks/**white socks**/white shoes
5.	camisa roja	**red shirt**/red skirt/blue skirt
6.	par de zapatos marrones	black socks/brown socks/**brown shoes**
7.	suéter violeta	**purple sweater**/purple jacket/pink sweater
8.	pantalones negros	brown pants/**black pants**/black shoes
9.	peinilla rosada	pink brush/pink T-shirt/**pink comb**
10.	cepillo marrón	brown toothbrush/**brown brush**/black brush

11.	vestido amarillo	yellow sweater/orange dress/**yellow dress**
12.	sudadera anaranjada	**orange sweatshirt**/yellow sweatshirt/ orange shirt
13.	mochila azul	green blouse/blue belt/**blue backpack**
14.	cepillo de dientes verde	green brush/red brush/**green toothbrush**
15.	falda anaranjada	**orange skirt**/yellow jacket/yellow skirt
16.	paraguas rojo	**red umbrella**/red brush/pink brush

Encourage students to use other items and colors they wish to add to the list. Verify the form of the color.

EXPANSION

Writing activity. Students make an original packing list of clothing and other items they might like to take on the homestay. Check for the correct form of the noun and the color. NOTE: **Paraguas** is the same in both the singular and plural. **Jeans** and **pantalones** are always plural.

EXPANSION

Additional matching. More creative or linguistically competent students might enjoy trying to make up a matching activity similar to the one in their book.

VARIATION

Do "puzzle phrases," for which students must figure out whether the speaker is talking about one or more than one. For example: Puzzle phrase = **Tengo los paraguas rojos** *(I have the red umbrellas).* Answer = More than one, because the color **rojo** ends in **s**.

EXPANSION

What Color Should You Pack? (BLM 2.4, 2.5, and 2.6) BLM 2.4 is a list of clothing and travel items with which students match the correct form of the color according to the roll of a die. BLM 2.5 is a die form with a color word written on each side.

Supplies: Scissors, glue or tape, copies of **BLM 2.4** and **BLM 2.5** for each student, plus enough extra copies of **BLM 2.5** to allow for errors in cutting and constructing

Allow ample time for this activity. Students will need time to cut out and construct the die and then to use it to fill in the information on **BLM 2.5**. After students have finished the activity, check to see that they have written the correct form of the color for each item of clothing. Choices of color, of course, will vary. Possibilities are **azul, verde, blanco/a, amarillo/a, rojo/a, negro/a.**

VARIATION

A variation on this activity is to use **BLM 2.6** (a blank die form) instead of **BLM 2.5**. Students write six words for clothing items on the six squares of the blank die and then roll both the color die and the clothing die to make lists of colored clothing. Teams play to see who can create and record the most combinations (correct color forms required, of course) within one minute. (The **BLM 2.6** die form is useful not only for this activity, but also for any others you might invent throughout the *¡Buen viaje!* program.)

H. MY JOURNAL

Explain to students that the journal entry is going to be their way of summarizing the material they have covered in each Element. Encourage as much use of the Spanish language as possible. Do not be overly concerned with accuracy. This is an entry-level experience, and its goal is to encourage and facilitate second language production. Using interlanguage (mixing English and Spanish) helps the learner move into fuller use of the target language.

If you are going to use this as an assessment tool, be very clear about your expectations with regard to content and accuracy. It is imperative to use the same mode for assessment as instruction. Do not teach one way and assess another. For example, much of the instruction has focused on language input through listening, speaking, and passive recognition of the target language. Your assessment should occur in exactly the same manner as the instruction.

The material in *¡Buen viaje!* is designed to develop only minimal skill in second language acquisition. The focus is on exploration of, and motivation to study, another language. Assessment should be authentic and ongoing. It should be used for the purpose of assisting students with their language development, not for grades. If you must give grades in your classes, you are encouraged to consider all aspects of students' behavior in the classroom, i.e., participation, cooperation, and willingness to learn.

TRIP PLANS

Picture card #3 "Calendar" may be used with this element.

Contents

1. **Communicative Functions:**

   Imparting personal/factual information (requesting, reporting, receiving, and processing information), socializing, describing

2. **Content and Language Skills:**

   Months; days of the week; dates; written numbers and numerals used with dates (**el nueve de mayo, el 9 de mayo, 9/5**); birthdays; personal information (address, name, age, color of eyes/hair)

3. **Culture:**

   Variations in passports, calendars/dates

4. **Teaching and Learning Strategies:**

   Surveying, organizing, prioritizing, listening selectively, grouping, playing games, observing critically

Additional Activity Suggestions (Extension and Interdisciplinary)

1. **Extensions**

   - Have students contact consulates for application forms and travel/general information.

   - Have students visit a local travel agent for brochures and travel information, including airfare and other travel costs.

   - Have students discuss differences between a visa and a passport.

   - Have students develop a birthday book of family and classmates.

2. **Mathematics**

   - Have students conduct surveys of other school groups (classes, clubs, teachers) or family members (including extended family) to find out birthdates, those who have passports, eye and hair colors, possessions, etc.

   - Have students calculate percentages on information from surveys.

   - Have students report on the historical use of calendars and methods for calculating dates, months, years, etc.

3. **Culture/Art**

   - Ask pairs or small groups of students to be responsible for making a new calendar for each month using a bulletin board area. Encourage them to use original artwork and to research special festivals and holidays. If they begin this project prior to covering the information in this Element, tell students to begin the week with Monday, as people do in countries where Spanish is spoken. Recognize birthdays of students in the class by noting them on the monthly calendar. You may also ask students to keep a smaller version designed on tagboard or poster board. This is also a good idea for teachers who do not have a permanent classroom.

5. **Advisor/Advisee or Homeroom**

   • Discuss birthdays and ages, leading into a discussion of the celebration of the **Quinceañera** in Spanish-speaking cultures. From this, move to a discussion of the "benchmarks" or "rites of passage" (legal age to drive, drink, etc.) in the culture of the United States.

Special Notes to the Teacher

In these materials you will see the use of three terms: *variation, expansion,* and *extension. Variation* activities are directly related to the information being presented and offer a slightly different perspective and/or option for presentation and/or practice. *Expansion* notes are also related directly to the information being presented and are intended to expand the material. *Extension* materials are those such as interdisciplinary activities that may be only tangentially related to the original material. Extension activities are a "spin-off" from the original and are intended to offer a variety of activities, including some which may not have language acquisition as a goal.

Things to Remember About Language Learning

If you have not already done so, you may want to discuss briefly the fact that Spanish is a phonetic language and that this can help students with pronunciation. Remind students about cognates and how these words can also be helpful to their understanding of the language. Encourage guessing and risk taking as this Element introduces more language. Resist the urge to overcorrect pronunciation and structure. Opt instead for a relaxed approach in which students are encouraged to have fun and experiment with the language.

In this Element you will find more use of *interlanguage* as a natural way to encourage second language development. Some activity direction lines will also give students the opportunity to use *subvocalization* as a building block to second language acquisition.

PERSPECTIVA

The **Perspectiva** is an advance organizer intended to stimulate discussion about the topic to be covered in this Element. Have students look at the picture of the passport. Ask if anyone in the class has a passport and, if so, why. Ask if anyone in their family or among their friends has a passport. Discuss the reasons for having passports. Focus on the passport dates and talk with students about how they will expand their ability to use numbers and to schedule events through understanding the use of months, days, and dates in Spanish.

If you have covered the first two Elements, briefly review the information and story line pertaining to preparations for the homestay. Encourage discussion about additional activities students might need to do to get ready for this imaginary trip. This is an excellent opportunity to talk about the value of planning and organization as a study and life skill.

VARIATION

BLM 3.0. Make a transparency of **BLM 3.0.** Use it to help students focus on the topics to be covered in this Element. This transparency may also be used as a culminating and/or assessment activity.

A replica of an actual passport application is provided in the Blackline Masters for this Element. This, as well as similar activities in subsequent Elements, gives the learner practical experience in following directions and filling out personal information forms.

A. MI AÑO ESCOLAR (MY SCHOOL YEAR)

Present the title of this activity. Remind students of cognates and how these words can be helpful to them in understanding the Spanish language. Alert them to the reverse position of the words for *school year*. Do not dwell on the grammatical concept of adjective placement. Go over the opening of the activity. Practice the question **¿Cómo se dice _____ en español?** This is a phrase that should be used frequently in the classroom as you encourage students to try to acquire new vocabulary in Spanish and to experiment with using the language. Present the word for *month*, **mes**, and the plural form **meses.** Again, do not dwell on grammatical concepts. Simply present the information in a manner appropriate to and commensurate with the age and developmental level of students.

Mention that, in Spanish, the names of the months as well as days of the week are not capitalized. Introduce the names of the months by modeling them in sequence beginning with January (**enero**). After you have modeled them several times, have students repeat the names after you. Then practice them in random order, for example: **mayo, octubre, marzo, septiembre, julio, diciembre, febrero, abril, noviembre, agosto, enero, junio.** Use abbreviations or a calendar in English for association until students become familiar with the sounds in Spanish.

VARIATION

Review new month vocabulary using the **cómo se dice** pattern. Have student(s) ask for the month in Spanish using this phrase.

Student: **¿Cómo se dice** *January* **en español?**

Teacher: **Se dice** *enero* **en español.**

VARIATION

Use the "pull it out of the bag" trick. Prepare individual flash cards with the names of months in Spanish on one side and English on the reverse side. Put these cards in a word box or bag. Have a student pull a vocabulary card from the word box or bag and ask, **¿Cómo se dice** *(April)* **en español?** Another student responds, *(April)* **se dice** *abril* **en español.**

VARIATION

Say the names of the months, asking students to listen carefully, focusing on the sound of their favorite (or birthday) month. Repeat the names of the months, this time having students raise their hands or stand up when they hear their favorite (or birthday) month. Ask for volunteers to tell why they like this month.

Say the names of the months and have students repeat them after you. Then tell them you will all do it again, but this time, when their favorite month is said, they should yell it aloud in Spanish. (Which month has the biggest cheering section?)

Finally, have students look at the school year planning calendar in their book. Go over the directions for this activity with them, allowing them to circle the months they recognize. Verify the first month of their school year and then have students complete the activity by writing the months on the calendar.

B. MI CUMPLEAÑOS (MY BIRTHDAY)

Review directions with students. Students should recognize **año** *(year)* as part of the word **cumpleaños**. Verify the writing of each student's birth month in the blank provided.

C. ENCUESTAS (SURVEYS)

Review directions with students. This activity has two parts, a survey of class-mates to be done during class and a survey of friends and family or others to be completed outside of class.

1. *Classmate Tally.* Have students circulate, do the survey, and then answer the questions. Limit time as appropriate to age and developmental level. Use a timer to indicate time. Follow up by doing the activity on an overhead transparency, on the chalkboard, or on newsprint so that students can check their own work.

2. *Ask Some Others.* Assign students the job of filling in the survey for home-work. In the next class period, have them report their findings.

INTERDISCIPLINARY EXTENSION

Mathematics Graphing. Write the months across the chalkboard. Give each student a small "post-it" note. Instruct students to put their birthdate and name on their "post-it." As you call out a month, have students whose birthday falls in that month come to the board and put their "post-it" under the name of the month. At the end, you will have a visual graph of birthdays in the class by month.

EXPANSION

Group the months by seasons and teach the names of the seasons, beginning with **primavera** *(spring),* **verano** *(summer),* **otoño** *(autumn),* **invierno** *(winter).*

EXPANSION

Teach the most common weather expressions for each of the months/seasons. (You can refer to Element 11 for weather vocabulary.)

D. LOS DÍAS DE LA SEMANA (DAYS OF THE WEEK)

Follow the same format and/or variations used for introducing months in Activity A. Begin with Monday (**lunes**), then say the days in sequence (**martes, miércoles, jueves, viernes, sábado, domingo**). Review the fact that Spanish speakers recognize the first day of the week as Monday (**lunes**) and the end of the week, or "weekend," as Saturday (**sábado**) and Sunday (**domingo**).

EXPANSION

Have students do a class survey (**una encuesta**). Tell students to write the days of the week down on the left side of a sheet of paper. Remind them to begin with **lunes** and not to capitalize the days. Then tell them they will take a class survey, or **una encuesta**. Explain that as you call a name (by roll/alphabetical order/drawing from a hat/etc.), each student will say his or her favorite day in Spanish. Tell students to listen carefully and keep track of the responses by placing hash marks after the days they have written on their paper, so that when they are done, they can tally the results. Show students how to tally groups of five by using vertical lines to count to four and then crossing them with a fifth line for five (卌). Do your own tally on a blank transparency. When the class is finished, project the results on the overhead and let students check their accuracy.

EXPANSION

BLM 3.1 and/or 3.2. Duplicate one copy of one (or both) puzzle(s) for each student. Be sure to point out the vocabulary clues at the bottom of 3.2.

E. LOS NÚMEROS (NUMBERS)

Refer students back to the calendar in Activity D. They should have put the current month in the top space and the days of the week (beginning with **lunes**) in the spaces below the name of the month. Review numbers from 1 to 10. Be sure students understand that the calendar they will now complete is to reflect the current month. Have them place the numerals 1 to 10 in the upper left corner of the appropriate squares on the calendar. Quiet counting to themselves as they write encourages language development through subvocalization.

HINT: Consult an early elementary teacher or a resource center for games and realia you can use to teach numbers. Materials that are not language specific (such as Cuisinaire rods) are excellent resources.

Introduce the numbers from 11 to 31. Use a variety of techniques to avoid rote memorization of the sequence. Examples follow:

1. Put the numerals in sequence on the board. Have students say or write out the appropriate number as you point to the numerals in random order.

2. Dictate numbers and have students write either the appropriate numeral or the spelled out number on a piece of paper. Verify answers after each number is read. You also can use the overhead projector and uncover each number after you have said it aloud. A student volunteer can also write on the overhead transparency, on newsprint, or on the chalkboard.

3. Have students make 5 × 7 cards using shirt cardboard or pieces of poster board or tagboard. Have them write one numeral on each card, large enough to be seen from the opposite end of the room. Tell them to hold their cards "playing card style" in their hands or to spread them on the desktop. As you or a student volunteer says a number in Spanish, students hold up the card showing the corresponding numeral. This can also be done as a timed small-group activity.

EXPANSION

Here are the words to the song "¡Cuenta!" This song is recorded on the Teacher Tape.

NOTE: The word **cuenta** *(count)* is used as a background vocal part.

¡Cuenta!
¡Uno, dos, tres, cuatro, cinco, seis, siete, ocho, nueve, diez!
¡Once, doce, trece, catorce, quince, dieciséis, diecisiete, dieciocho, diecinueve, veinte!
¡Veintiuno, veintidós, veintitrés, veinticuatro, veinticinco, veintiséis, veintisiete, veintiocho, veintinueve, treinta!

From: *Sing, Dance, Laugh, and Eat Tacos!* by Barbara MacArthur
copyright 1990, 6945 Hwy. 14 East, Janesville, WI 53546.

F. LA FECHA (THE DATE)

Use the realia pictured. Ask students to discuss the dates they see on each item. Lead them to note the reversed order of the month and day. Go over the dates listed in the activity, saying them in Spanish. Students practice by repeating after you. Allow time for pair practice. Then have them complete the activity as directed.

Answer Key:

1. E   July 25th

2. G   April 1st

3. B   December 25th

4. C   March 12th

5. H   September 15th

6. F   October 12th

7. D   May 1st

8. A   February 15th

Discuss how to talk about the "first" of the month—how it is expressed in English and how it is expressed in Spanish. You may want to explain briefly the difference between cardinal and ordinal numbers.

Have students write the answer to the question. How do Spanish speakers write **primero** as a numeral? 1º

G. LA FECHA ESCRITA EN NÚMEROS (THE DATE IN NUMERALS)

Go through the dates expressed only in numerals, reading them a loud in Spanish. Be sure students notice how the order of the information is different from the usual sequence in the United States. Then have students take turns saying their birth date in English. Ask individuals to come to the board and write the Spanish numeral version for the class.

Have each student write his or her own birth date in the space provided in the book, and when that has been done, have students exchange books with a partner and complete the activity by writing the partner's date in words.

CONTEXTUALIZED PRACTICE
Review the directions and the example with students. Allow ample time for students to complete the activity individually or in pairs. Verify responses by placing answers on the chalkboard or overhead.

1. February 10   10/4   el diez de abril
2. March 1   1/5   el primero de mayo
3. July 7   7/9   el siete de septiembre
4. October 30   30/12   el treinta de diciembre
5. August 29   29/10   el veintiuno de octubre
6. April 25   25/6   el veinticinco de junio
7. June 13   13/8   el trece de agosto

H. DOS PASAPORTES (TWO PASSPORTS)

Discuss passports with students. Refer back to discussion of the **Perspectiva** and/or look again at that page. Go over the two passports and introduce the vocabulary associated with the information they contain. Encourage students to guess and to refer to their knowledge of cognates.

Vocabulary:

pasaporte	passport
apellido	last name
nombre	first name
fecha de nacimiento	date of birth
dirección	address
teléfono	telephone
color del pelo	hair color
color de los ojos	eye color
negro(s)	black
nombres de padres	parents' names

Answer Key:

1. Apellido	¿de Kristina?	Sullivan
	¿de Enrique?	Carmona
2. Fecha de nacimiento	¿de Kristina?	el 7 de septiembre, 1983 / *September 7, 1983*
	¿de Enrique?	el 27 de marzo, 1983 / *March 27, 1983*
3. Teléfono	¿de Kristina?	313-296-4157
	¿de Enrique?	5-521-79-53
4. Color de los ojos	¿de Kristina?	verdes / *green*
	¿de Enrique?	negros / *black*
5. Dirección	¿de Kristina?	36570 Utica Road, Summerville, Michigan 48096, U.S.A.
	¿de Enrique?	27 Independencia, México, D. F., México

Answer Key:

1. d. 27/3/83

2. a. Sullivan

3. c. 313-296-4157

4. b. negro

5. c. 27 Independencia

I. SOLICITUD PARA MI PASAPORTE (APPLICATION FOR MY PASSPORT)

Part 1.

Duplicate enough copies of the passport application (**BLM 3.3**) for each student to have one. Make extra copies to allow for errors. Guide students through the process of completing the application. Your involvement in this activity will be more or less important depending upon the age and developmental level of students. This is another opportunity to assist students in learning an important survival skill for the real world. You may also want to have them compare the information requested with the passport information/vocabulary from Activity H. Allow ample time for completion of the activity.

Part 2.

Supplies needed: Paper, marking pens/crayons, stapler
Duplicate sufficient copies of the mock passport cover and inside pages (**BLM 3.4 and BLM 3.5**). Have students cut out and construct the passport and then fill in the information. This activity will also serve to review vocabulary from the earlier parts of the Element.

Once the passports are made, divide the class into two groups—travelers and passport control agents. Assign a different country to each agent. Travelers greet the agent by saying **Buenos días.** The agent answers and writes on the mock passport the name of the country and the date of entry using the Spanish order of day/month. Each subsequent agent must use a date later than the previous one. Travelers circulate around the room until they have "visited" several different countries and obtained the control agent's "stamp." Set a specific number of countries they should visit. Then have students switch roles and do the activity again. When the whole class has visited the assigned number of countries, ask students to compile a travel log of their journey by indicating each country, date of entry in numeral form, and date of entry in words (for example: **España, 25/5, el veinticinco de mayo**).

J. MI DIARIO (MY JOURNAL)

Explain to students that the journal entry is going to be their way of summarizing the material they have covered in each Element. Encourage as much use of the Spanish language as possible. Do not be overly concerned with accuracy. This is an entry-level experience, and its goal is to encourage and facilitate second language production. Using interlanguage (mixing English and Spanish) helps the learner move into fuller use of the target language.

If you are going to use this as an assessment tool, be very clear about your expectations with regard to content and accuracy. It is imperative to use the same mode for assessment as instruction. Do not teach one way and assess another.

For example, much of the instruction has focused on language input through listening, speaking, and passive recognition of the target language. Your assessment should occur in exactly the same manner as the instruction. Suggestion: Give students a blank passport or passport application in Spanish. Have them complete the required information in Spanish with their own or imaginary information. For example, **Apellido** followed by a blank should elicit a last (family) name, such as Anderson. **Nombre** should elicit a first (given) name, such as Janet.

The material in *¡Buen viaje!* is designed to develop only minimal skill in second language acquisition. The focus is on exploration of, and motivation to study, another language. Assessment should be authentic and ongoing. It should be used for the purpose of assisting students with their language development, not for grades. If you must give grades in your classes, you are encouraged to consider all aspects of students' behavior in the classroom, i.e., participation, cooperation, and willingness to learn.

4 TRAVEL DETAILS

Picture card #4 "Boy with family" may be used with this element.

Contents

1. **Communicative Functions:**

   Expressing and finding out emotional/intellectual attitudes (liking and disliking), imparting and seeking factual information (reporting, asking)

2. **Content and Language Skills:**

   Me gusta/No me gusta, personal information (address, telephone number, family, pets), recreational activities and sports, telling time (on the hour)

3. **Culture:**

   Appropriate exchange of personal information

4. **Teaching and Learning Strategies:**

   Organizing, webbing thematically, calculating, filling out forms

Additional Activity Suggestions (Extension and Interdisciplinary)

1. **Mathematics**

   • Have students research prices of airline tickets to Spanish-speaking countries. Have them also check travel restrictions, times, price variations, connections, etc.

   • Have students calculate time-zone differences around the world and construct graphs and charts to show these differences (labeled in Spanish, if possible).

2. **Social Studies**

   • Have students investigate various resources and activities available in the community for an exchange/homestay student.

   • Have students research the difference between passports and visas for travel.

   • Have students interview members of the community who may come from Spanish-speaking countries. Create a list of pertinent information regarding differences in leisure activities/pastimes.

3. **Economics**

   • Invite a local banker to visit your class to explain the federal banking system.

   • Have students investigate electronic transfer of funds.

   • Take a field trip to a local bank/credit union.

   • Obtain information on international banking, including job opportunities.

4. **Health/Physical Education**

- Have students discuss the notion of "jet lag." Ask them to discuss how this affects people who travel across time zones. What are some suggested remedies to counteract this phenomenon?

- Have students look at the list of sports/activities and discuss the importance of physical fitness.

5. **Advisor/Advisee or Homeroom**

- Discuss the importance of completing forms accurately.

- Ask students to role-play meeting new acquaintances. Follow up with a discussion of the importance of first impressions.

- Form cooperative learning groups to plan short lessons on organizing and planning time to complete tasks.

- Encourage discussion of whether cooperating with others gets things done more efficiently and effectively.

Special Notes to the Teacher

In these materials you will see the use of three terms: *variation, expansion,* and *extension. Variation* activities are directly related to the information being presented and offer a slightly different perspective and/or option for presentation and/or practice. *Expansion* notes are also related directly to the information being presented and are intended to expand the material. *Extension* materials are those such as interdisciplinary activities that may be only tangentially related to the original material. Extension activities are a "spin-off" from the original and are intended to offer a variety of activities, including some which may not have language acquisition as a goal.

Element 4 offers numerous opportunities to discuss the value of planning, organization, and efficient use of time in daily life. Schedules, lists, and sharing responsibility to accomplish tasks are an integral part of the material presented. Help your students view the activities from two levels: 1) accomplishing the tasks outlined in the activities and 2) applying these same skills elsewhere.

PERSPECTIVA

The **Perspectiva** is an advance organizer intended to stimulate discussion about the topics to be covered in this Element. Ask the class to look at the picture. Students should focus on telling time and filling out personal information forms. Review the vocabulary word **pasaporte** and the expression **¡Vámonos!**

VARIATION

BLM 4.0. Make a transparency of BLM 4.0. Use it to help students focus on the topics to be covered in this Element. This transparency may also be used as a culminating and/or assessment activity.

A. FORMULARIO DE DATOS PERSONALES

The Personal Information Form in this first activity has two separate parts. You may, if you wish, present the entire activity first and then work separately with each part.

In the first part, if students have pets other than those mentioned on the form, help them find the word in a Spanish-English dictionary and make an additional blank on the form and draw or cut out a picture of that pet.

The vocabulary in Element 4 can be used to introduce a number of grammar points (**mi/mis** for possessives and plurals; **hermano(s)/hermana(s)** for masculine/feminine and plurals). Avoid making grammar the primary focus and present the words as lexical items. The concept of masculine and feminine forms of nouns and adjectives was introduced with adjectives of color in Element 2. If it seems appropriate and contributes to students' understanding of the new vocabulary, remind them of this previously presented material. If students do not raise the question, then treat the terms as separate lexical items. Make minimal reference to grammatical concepts. Present them only if they are developmentally appropriate to your students. Abstract grammar concepts are difficult, if not meaningless, to many transescent learners.

Refer to Element 3 for the introduction of the phrase **¿Cómo se dice _____ en español?** Use the phrase to review vocabulary from previous Elements and as a means to present new vocabulary items.

Go through the directions for the activity with the class. Now that students are preparing for the homestay, tell them that they are going to send information about themselves to their host family. Ask if they recognize any words from the passport activity in Element 3 (**Apellido, Teléfono, Dirección**). Review the form and encourage students to circle any words they do not understand and to guess what those words mean.

Before working with the second section of the form, ask students to bring in pictures of the activities and sports mentioned. Put a list on the chalkboard, on the bulletin board, and/or on newsprint. Allow students to sign up or volunteer to find certain pictures in magazines or catalogues. Another option is to collect old magazines/catalogues in the classroom and give students time to cut and paste flash cards using heavy construction paper, poster board, or tagboard. Squares made from shirt cardboard also work well.

VARIATION

Use 3 X 5 index cards to practice the vocabulary. Have students cut out a picture or draw an object representing the activity or sport and put it on one side of the card. The vocabulary word or phrase is written on the opposite side (examples: musical note/**escuchar la música**, book/**leer**, airplane/**viajar**). Have students work in pairs with their cards. Student A holds up a card. Student B replies, **Me gusta _____** or **No me gusta _____**.

VARIATION

Have students make flash cards showing pictures of the equipment used for each sport. The sport is written on the back of the card. Working in pairs, have students practice giving the name of the sport when the picture of the equipment is shown.

EXPANSION

Have students work in pairs or small groups to create a matching activity using pictures/drawings and the Spanish words/phrases. This may be done on a large poster board. Students should match sports figures from around the world to their sport, the equipment to the sport, or a combination of the people and the equipment. Use push pins and strands of colored yarn or twine to extend a line from one item to the correct match. (Colored yarn can also be a way of reviewing colors from Element 2.)

EXTENSION

Encuestas. Use the same suggestions that were used for determining birthdays and favorite days of the week in Element 3. Students can make charts and/or graphs depicting the favorite sports and activities of class members.

B. LLENAR EL FORMULARIO

¿**Listo?** *(Ready?)* is used when speaking to one person. ¿**Listos?** is used when speaking with more than one person.

Referring back to Kristina Sullivan's Personal Information Form (Activity A), have each student complete his or her own form.

C. ORGANIZACIÓN PARA EL VIAJE

Remind students about cognates (Element 1) when they look at **verdadero** and **falso**. Review the days of the week from Element 3. If necessary, complete any of the suggested activities from that Element that you have not covered or wish to repeat. Talk with students about the importance of organizing their time and activities. Relate this to travel, but also to school work, responsibilities at home, and preparation for the world of work. Go over the preparations done by Kristina. If students are not familiar with traveler's checks, bring in an actual sample of a traveler's check. Explain the reason for using these checks.

Answer Key:

1. verdadero
2. falso
3. falso
4. verdadero
5. verdadero
6. falso

EXTENSION

Have students go to a bank or credit union and purchase traveler's checks. This may not be appropriate for younger students; however, older students could go with a parent/teacher chaperon.

INTERDISCIPLINARY EXTENSION

Mathematics. Find the rate of exchange for the currency of one country. Have students make a list of several items they might need or want to purchase during their homestay and calculate the amount in the foreign currency (example: toothbrush, toothpaste, T-shirt, notebook).

D. ORGANIZACIÓN DE LA SEMANA

Read the directions with the class. Allow them to create their own specific and special tasks using the blank post-it notes.

E. COMPARAR ENTRE AMIGOS

This activity may be done in pairs or small groups. Encourage students to discuss the rationale for their choice of day. Help them look for a logical and appropriate sequencing of tasks.

F. ¿QUÉ HORA ES?

Review the numbers from 1 to 31 with the class (see Element 3). Draw a circle on the chalkboard or on an overhead transparency. A cardboard clock with moveable hands is also a good tool. Make your own according to the directions to students in Activity G, or purchase one of these clocks at a teacher supply store. Set your demonstration clock at a given hour and model the time by saying the time in Spanish. Avoid using 1:00 and 12:00 until students become familiar with giving the time on the hour with all of the other numerals. Then introduce **es el mediodía, es la medianoche** with a brief explanation of the difference in the way these hours are expressed. Point out the similar difference in the English forms *noon* and *midnight*. Finally, unless you want to wait for students to figure it out as they do the activity, present 1:00 (**Es la una**).

VARIATION

Draw circles on the board and letter them the same way they are lettered in the text. Point randomly to a clock, saying, **¿Qué hora es?** Students call out the time in Spanish. Also, do this rapidly by just pointing to the clocks in random order until students can easily say the time of day in Spanish. Include noon, midnight, and 1:00 in this drill. (Distinguish 12:00 A.M and P.M. by putting a star and moon next to midnight and a sun with rays next to noon.)

Answer Key:

1. C
2. B
3. F
4. G
5. A
6. E
7. D
8. H
9. D, H

1:00 is **Es la una**.

It is different because the other numbers are plural (more than one).

    If developmentally appropriate at this point, talk briefly about the two forms **es** and **son**. Present them as lexical items and not as the grammatical concept of irregular verb forms.

G. UN RELOJ

Assemble all materials necessary for making clocks. Allow ample time for the activity and encourage students to be creative as they decorate the clock faces. When the students are finished, say times on the hour in Spanish. Tell students to move the hands to indicate the time of day you mentioned and hold up the clock or show the clock to you or a partner. Give a preparatory phrase before you actually give the time: for example, *Ready?* (¿Listos?) Then proceed with times from 2:00 to 11:00 in random order. Avoid using 1:00, midnight, and noon at first. Include them only after other times have been practiced. Students should leave their clocks in the classroom for future activities.

PARTNER ACTIVITY

Allow time for students to work in pairs according to the instructions. Circulate around the room as the activity progresses.

EXPANSION

Have pairs or small groups work together to make extra clocks to be used if a student breaks his or her clock or takes it from the classroom.

H. ¿A QUÉ HORA?

Go over the directions for this activity with the class. Tell students that you are going to read each activity on the grid followed by the time of day it takes place. First, read only the activities. Have students repeat them after you. Do the first one as an example, and check to be sure everyone knows the procedure. Then complete the exercise. Read each activity and time twice, pausing briefly between each reading. When you have completed all the items, read the times back and have students correct their answers. You may also call for volunteers and have them read the times back to you "bingo style" individually or together.

Script:

1.	ir de compras	a las dos	(2:00)
2.	ir a un concierto	a las cuatro	(4:00)
3.	ir a un museo	a las tres	(3:00)
4.	ir a un partido de fútbol	a las siete	(7:00)
5.	comer	a las diez	(10:00)
6.	ir a la escuela	a las ocho	(8:00)
7.	jugar al tenis	a las cinco	(5:00)
8.	hablar por teléfono	a las seis	(6:00)
9.	ir al cine	a las nueve	(9:00)

VARIATION

Make an overhead transparency of the grid. Have one or more students do the exercise on the transparency with the projector light off (or at their desk). At the end of the exercise, show the transparency on the projector and correct the grid as a group. Use only volunteers for this type of activity.

VARIATION

Have a grid prepared on the overhead with the answers marked. At the end of your dictation, turn on the projector light and allow students to check their papers.

VARIATION

Have students work in pairs and dictate to each other. Give them a list of times to use or have them make up their own lists.

INTERDISCIPLINARY EXTENSION

Social Studies: Time Zones. Have an atlas available in the room and point out different time zones to students. Show them that as you move toward the east, the time is later. Start with 11:00 A.M. in Los Angeles and ask students to tell you what time it would be in the following cities: Denver (12:00 noon), Chicago (1:00 P.M.), New York (2:00 P.M.). Ask students to find out how many hours of time difference there are between New York and Madrid (New York is six hours earlier). Next, present a city and a time: **En Chicago son las tres.** Follow by asking **¿Qué hora es en New York?** A student answers **En New York, son las dos.** Continue with other cities and times.

This same exercise can be done using the clock faces. Instead of answering orally, students simply set the time on their clocks. The times may also be written on a piece of paper and checked as you progress through the activity.

You may also choose to do a number of nonlanguage activities with time zones and the concept of intercontinental travel.

I. ETIQUETA DE EQUIPAJE

Review the instructions with the class. Each student should then complete his or her own tag. This is a good culminating activity that may also be used for assessment. You can verify students' reading comprehension of items to be completed. Since this involves personal information, there is little or no chance for error in the completion of the items, thereby ensuring success for virtually all students.

J. MI DIARIO

Remind students that the journal entry is going to be their way of summarizing the material they have covered in this Element. In an exploratory experience, one of the goals is to facilitate second language acquisition. Encourage students to use as much Spanish as possible. Do not be overly concerned with accuracy. Using interlanguage (natural mixing of words known in Spanish with English) helps the learner move into fuller use of the target language.

The **Mi diario** activity is a culminating writing activity. If you are going to use it as an assessment tool, tell students exactly what is expected with regard to format, content, and accuracy. It is imperative to use the same mode for assessment as instruction. Do not teach one way and assess another. For example, much of the instruction has focused on language input through listening, speaking, and passive recognition of the target language. Your assessment should occur in exactly the same manner as the instruction. Suggestion: Give students a blank **Formulario de datos personales.** Have them complete the form with their own personal information. For example, **Apellido** followed by a blank should elicit a last (family) name such as Anderson, **Nombre,** a first (given) name such as Janet.

EXCHANGING LETTERS WITH YOUR HOST FAMILY

Picture cards 5a "Family" and 5b "Boy wrapping present" may be used with this element.

Contents

1. **Communicative Functions:**

   Expressing and finding out emotional and intellectual attitudes, imparting and seeking factual information

2. **Content and Language Skills:**

   Numbers 10 to 1,000, understanding and giving addresses and telephone numbers (international), vocabulary associated with a letter of personal introduction (family, pets, likes/dislikes), writing a personal letter of introduction, addressing an envelope, adjective agreement using adjectives of personality and personal characteristics

3. **Culture:**

   International addresses and telephone numbers, exchange of appropriate personal information, gift giving for hospitality

4. **Teaching and Learning Strategies:**

   Developing letter-writing skills, utilizing self-reflection, discussing personality traits of self and others, organizing, webbing thematically

Additional Activity Suggestions (Extension and Interdisciplinary)

1. **Extensions**

   - Contact pen pal organizations and begin a letter exchange.

   - Have students look up additional names of animals as household pets and make a poster or collage of pictures of these animals and label them in Spanish.

   - Have students look up Spanish names of animals other than pets. Then take a field trip to a pet store, zoo, or farm. Identify the animals, using Spanish words.

   - Arrange for an international operator to visit the class and discuss the process of making international telephone calls.

   - Invite a telephone company representative to talk about and demonstrate telephone, telegraph, fax, and fiber-optic networks.

2. **Science/Biology**

   - Have students research information on animals considered endangered species.

   - Do a webbing activity using the theme of animals. Webs might include habitats, number of feet, and carnivores.

3. **Language Arts**
   - Practice the correct forms for writing personal letters (formal and informal) and business letters.

4. **Advisor/Advisee or Homeroom**
   - Discuss the concept of "first impressions." Talk about the factors that contribute to first impressions, such as good grooming, polite speech, and behavior.

   - Review the adjectives used to describe personality traits and personal characteristics in Activity H. Talk about what they mean and how people exhibit these various traits.

   - Discuss the positive traits students recognize in themselves and others.

Special Notes to the Teacher

The amount of Spanish vocabulary increases substantially in this Element. There is more of the target language used in the activities as well as in their titles. Continue to encourage students to guess the meanings of new words and phrases from context. Direct them to pictures, drawings, and themes to help derive the English meanings. When the new vocabulary includes verb forms, they should be presented as lexical items with minimal reference to grammar.

PERSPECTIVA

The **Perspectiva** is an advance organizer intended to stimulate discussion about the topic to be covered in this Element. Focus discussion on letters and pictures as a way of exchanging information. Have students look at the pictures and guess what information will be exchanged (family members, pets, sports and other activities).

VARIATION

BLM 5.0. Make a transparency of **BLM 5.0.** Use it to help students focus on the topics to be covered in this Element. This transparency may also be used as a culminating and/or assessment activity.

COOPERATIVE LEARNING EXTENSION

Mobile. This team-building activity can serve as an opportunity to teach basic shapes as an expansion activity: **triángulo**/triangle, **cuadrado**/square, **rectángulo**/rectangle, **círculo**/circle. Have students make a mobile of themselves and their family, friends, and pets. Use coat hangers, construction paper, glue, fishing line or thread, and markers. Take Polaroid pictures of the students. Have students cut geometric shapes out of construction paper, mount their picture on the contruction paper, and attach the picture to the coat hanger with fishing line or thread. Students can also bring in pictures of their family, friends, and pets. They can mount these pictures on construction paper and add them to their mobile. Label the pictures with Spanish names. Suspend the mobiles from the ceiling in the classroom.

Construct the mobile, using favorite pets or activities as the subject.

Class Tree

Decorate a classroom bulletin board with a large tree. Take Polaroid pictures of students. Cut out leaf forms from construction paper. Mount the student pictures on the leaves. The trunk, made from construction paper, is labeled with the school name, **Clase de español**, or **Clase de Sra./Sr./Srta.** _____.

VARIATION

Use class subjects as the tree leaves. Draw symbols to depict class content as the leaves.

A. LOS NÚMEROS DE 10 A 1.000

HINT: Consult an early elementary teacher or resource center for games and realia you can use to teach numbers. Materials that are not language specific (such as Cuisinaire rods) are excellent resources. Point out to students that in Spanish-speaking countries, the higher numbers use a period instead of a comma. Tell them they may also see an extra space utilized to separate the numerals.

Begin with a brief review of the numbers 1 to 31 (see Element 3). Utilize any of the suggestions in that Element to introduce and practice the numbers 10 to 1,000. Go over the directions for the activity with the class. Then model the numbers by counting aloud while students count quietly to themselves. Count by tens from 10 to 100 and then by hundreds from 100 to 1,000. Be sure students understand that Spanish speakers write numbers of 1,000 or more with a period or a space instead of a comma.

Ask for volunteers to write the numerals and words on the board. Form a circle around the room. Have a student in the circle say **diez** and call out another student's name. That second student then gives the next number up by 10 (**veinte**) and calls out a third student's name, who should say **treinta** and the name of a fourth student. Continue this round-robin practice counting from 100 to 1,000 by hundreds. If a student forgets a number, he or she may use the board for a quick hint.

Especially in the initial stages of the process, allow peer coaching. It creates an atmosphere of cooperation and collaboration and lessens the competitive nature of the classroom. Middle-level learners need the support of their peers. If the class is too large to form a circle, divide the class in half. Those students who remain seated should write the numbers on a piece of paper or otherwise practice actively in their places. Once students become comfortable and knowledgeable with the numbers, you can time the activity. For example, students must respond within 20 seconds or lose their turn.

VARIATION

Have students toss a Nerf ball from one student to the next. Whoever catches the ball counts out loud.

VARIATION

Students count by tens starting with 15 (15, 25, 35, etc.), instead of the usual 10, 20, 30. It's more challenging. They can also count by tens starting with 12 (12, 22, 32, etc.).

B. DIRECCIÓN Y NÚMERO DE TELÉFONO DE MI FAMILIA

Review the activity with students by going over the list of names and addresses. Students can refer to information in Element 1 about the cities and countries where the host families are located. Each student should select a homestay family. Encourage students to identify with their chosen family. Tell them that they will be using this family name, address, and telephone number in future activities.

NOTA: Review the information in the **NOTA** with students. Go over the questions that follow it and ask students to answer, based on the family they have chosen.

EXPANSION

Have students go back through the host family list and give the country code for each entry.

INTERDISCIPLINARY EXTENSION

Social Studies. Have students research family names. They can do this for Spanish names or their own. This is a good multicultural activity, particularly if you have a variety of ethnic names and backgrounds represented in the class. It is interesting for students to explore the meaning and trace the origin of their family names.

C. CARTA Y SOBRE

Have students use the name and address of the family they selected in Activity B. Encourage them to use good penmanship. Talk about the correct form for address and return address on an envelope.

D. LA CARTA DE KRISTINA

Remind students that Kristina is a student who went on the homestay last year. They will be using her experiences and information as a reference. This is a reading activity. It is imperative that students understand that they are to read for general comprehension. Walk them through the three-step process of reading: 1) for general meaning, 2) for more detail and to focus on vocabulary, and 3) for further detail and practice.

Review the vocabulary with students. Introduce each word and phrase as a lexical item. **Soy,** for example, should be presented as the Spanish equivalent for the English *I am* or *I'm*, and not as a verb form. Some of the items can be presented and practiced using Total Physical Response (TPR) (for example: **nadar, jugar al tenis, entusiasmado/a**). Wherever possible, use visuals and realia: a tennis racket, a stuffed toy dog, a miniature house, or pictures of these items. Always introduce and practice vocabulary in a meaningful context. Do not have students write and memorize lists of Spanish words with their English meanings. Encourage correct spelling; however, be more concerned with comprehension and correct use. Seek gradual error elimination as students progress.

This activity also uses **estoy** *(I am)*. Introduce this as a lexical item. If an explanation of the difference between **soy** and **estoy** is required, tell students that **estoy** is used when you describe yourself the way you are "sometimes" (happy, sad, talkative, etc.) and that **soy** is used to describe permanent characteristics (American, tall, brown-eyed, etc.).

E. TU CARTA

Remind students of the two different forms (masculine and feminine) of articles used in Spanish (Element 2). **Entusiasmada** was introduced in Activity D with an "a" ending because Kristina was talking about herself. Male students should use the form ending in "o." Have students guess what would happen to the form of the word if two females were describing themselves, or two males. Explain that if you have one male and one female, you use the "o" form, adding an **s** for the plural (**entusiasmados**).

This is a guided writing activity incorporating process writing techniques and practices. Peer correction and collaboration should be encouraged. Read through the letter with the class. Clarify any questions regarding the kind of information that should be supplied in each blank. Have students refer to Kristina's letter if they have questions. Students should use the outline in the book to write their first draft. They should work with a partner to correct and modify each other's letter, making any corrections and alterations next to or above the original in the text. A final draft should be completed on a clean sheet of paper. If students have access to computers, have them create the letter using the computer. Put final copies on the bulletin board.

VARIATION

Make an overhead transparency of the outline. Talk the class through the letter before they begin writing. Ask if someone would like to volunteer to do his or her first draft on the transparency. Use this as an example and correct the letter as a group. It is extremely important in this kind of activity that students view correction as a cooperative venture and not as criticism. Never insist that a student do his or her work for the entire class unless he or she volunteers to do so.

EXTENSION

Contact pen pals and have students begin individual or class correspondence with students in Spanish-speaking countries.

EXTENSION

Video letter. After students have composed their letters, make a video of students reading or reciting the letter. This is an excellent activity as a precursor to an actual exchange program.

INTERDISCIPLINARY EXTENSION

E-Mail. If your students have access to computers, work with a teacher in another school. Students communicate with each other via electronic mail, using the computer. Communication may be with other schools in your district or with another district in the same or another state.

F. LA RESPUESTA

Be sure that students understand the meaning of the activity title **La respuesta** (*The response*) and that this is a reading activity. Go over the letter with the class. Use the same procedures as Activity D.

G. FOTOS DE LA FAMILIA

Vocabulary: the possessive use of **de**
Present the activity title and subtitles as lexical items, not as grammar concepts. **Fotos de la familia** can be presented as meaning *Family pictures* or *Pictures of the family*. Present **La familia de Alejandro** as *Alejandro's family* and **Los amigos de Alejandro** as *Alejandro's friends*.

Review the activity and pictures with the class. Students then complete the activity as directed.

H. PRIMERA IMPRESIÓN

Most of the words presented are cognates. Encourage students to guess the meanings. Words with which they might need help are the following:

cariñoso(a), loving or kind/caring

egoísta, selfish

envidioso(a), jealous

hablador(a), talkative

perezoso(a), lazy

simpático(a), nice

trabajador(a), hardworking or industrious

valiente, brave

Discuss the sayings "One picture is worth a thousand words" and "Looks can be deceiving." Remind students of the **o** and **a** forms of words used to describe people and things. If they have done Element 2, remind them that they learned about these forms using color words in Element 2. They also learned the two forms of **entusiasmado/a** in Activities D and E of this Element.

This activity presents adjectives useful in describing individuals and their personalities. A word of caution! As you present the vocabulary and students use it, accentuate the positive! Middle-level learners are extremely sensitive and can also be cruel to their peers. Maintain an atmosphere that is positive and fosters a spirit of mutual support, cooperation, and collaboration. Never allow negative comments to be made about members of the class or others.

VARIATION

Use pictures of animals or actual stuffed animals to practice the vocabulary. Assign some of the more negative traits to animals (example: parrot = **hablador**, sloth = **perezoso**).

Have students fill in each blank under the pictures with one of the vocabulary words. Confirm that they have used the correct form.

I. IMPRESIONES

Vocabulary: **es** = is or he is/she is/it is. Introduce this word as a lexical item, not as a verb form.

Continue reinforcement and practice of the vocabulary from Activity H. This activity offers an opportunity for self-reflection. Encourage students to think in terms of their positive characteristics. Building self-esteem is particularly important for the transescent learner.

Help students identify individuals who they know and respect. Ask them to be clear about the reasons why they have selected these individuals. Have an English-Spanish dictionary handy for students who want to use an adjective that was not presented in Activity H.

EXPANSION

Use hand puppets to depict the various traits. Have students create short dialogues in which the puppets talk about themselves using the vocabulary from this Element. An example follows:

Puppet 1:   Me llamo Enrique. Tengo doce años. Soy valiente.

Puppet 2:   Me llamo Gloria. Me gusta jugar al tenis. Soy activa.

Puppet 3:   Me llamo Luís. Estudio español. No soy perezoso. Soy trabajador.

EXPANSION

Many adolescents are focused on sports and/or entertainment figures. Ask students to think about some admirable traits of these individuals. Many of these persons, for example, contribute to charity and charitable causes through concerts and athletic games to benefit health causes, the United Nations Children's Fund (UNICEF), recording royalties to environmental causes such as the rain forests, etc. Have students bring in newspaper or magazine articles illustrating ways in which such public figures contribute to society.

INTERDISCIPLINARY EXTENSION

Art. Have students draw caricatures or "smiley" faces and label them in Spanish to illustrate the vocabulary words.

J. UN REGALO

Review the activity with the class. Mention that it is considered polite to bring a small gift when visiting or staying in someone's home. This is true of the United States as well as other countries. Point out that more relaxed lifestyles in the United States do not always follow this protocol. Note, however, that in many other countries it would be considered grossly impolite to neglect to bring a gift.

COOPERATIVE LEARNING

Word Web Brainstorm. Remind the class that in a brainstorm activity any and all suggestions are acceptable. Have students complete the cells. If they wish to create other webs, allow them to do so. After completing the webs, they should try to reach a consensus. Talk about the process of reaching consensus. Be sure students understand that not everyone's ideas can be a final choice; however, all ideas are incorporated into the consensus building process. The goal is to reach a point where the majority of the students' suggestions are considered in a manner that is best for all. This may involve compromise!

K. MI DIARIO

Have old magazines and catalogues available to use for pictures of the **regalo.** Refer to previous Elements for suggestions and ideas about using this **Mi diario** activity. Encourage students to use as much Spanish as possible. This activity should be creative and fun!

**6**

PREPARING A PHOTO ALBUM

Picture cards 6a "Photo album" and 6b "Showing album" may be used with this element.

Special Notes to the Teacher

Remember that *¡Buen viaje!* is intended to be an initiation to other languages and cultures. The activities in each Element focus on cultural awareness, limited second language acquisition, and the development of practical life skills.

One of the goals of *¡Buen viaje!* is to have every student experience success in second language learning. All students are not expected to learn exactly the same content. They are, however, expected to participate in each of the activities of each Element to the level of their individual abilities. Students will demonstrate a variety and range of language proficiencies.

Element 6 is designed to address this range of proficiencies. The culminating activities offer multiple opportunities for expression. Options for using a variety of learning styles and modalities, as well as multiple cognitive approaches are provided. To facilitate teacher assessment, an Organization and Assessment Chart has been provided as a Blackline Master (BLM 6.1). This Organization and Assessment Chart is meant to be only one of many methods of assessment. It may be used by both the student and the teacher as a guideline to collaboratively assess the student's work.

Levels of Assessment:

Learning a language is not a linear event. Language develops globally and holistically. It is an experiential process. Watch how an infant develops his or her own first language. Observe the linguistic struggles of those individuals who have come to the United States with little or no functional ability in English. Reflect on your own experiences learning another language. Learning is most likely to occur when taking risks, using one's imagination, and being creative are encouraged. Students will manifest different levels of each of these qualities. In teaching this exploratory class, your role as a language teacher is to encourage risk taking in communicative situations. Use multiple teaching strategies and creative methods designed to enhance opportunities for communication and language learning.

Element 6 of the Student Manual gives students a format that they may use to prepare a photo album. It is designed as a minimal outcome for students in this course. Depending on the individual student's level of language proficiency and/or enthusiasm, you may choose to provide students with a more independent student-generated language assessment model that uses **el álbum** as the theme.

PERSPECTIVA

The **Perspectiva** is intended as an advance organizer to stimulate discussion about the topics to be covered in this Element. Element 6 is designed as a review of Elements 1 to 5. There are few new vocabulary items introduced in Element 6. Ask students to look at the picture of the album's title page (use a transparency of **BLM 6.0** if you wish). Help them recall the various topics and activities they have learned about to prepare for their imaginary homestay experience. Tell them that this Element will give them a chance to review the Spanish they have learned and to recall information they have gained about Spanish-speaking people and countries. They will review by constructing a photo album to show their host family and new friends. Emphasize that there is no single, correct, or "right" way to compile this album.

If you plan to use the Organization and Assessment Chart, distribute copies of the chart and discuss it with students. Be clear about your expectations regarding each of the items on the chart. Point out to students that while accuracy is always a goal, you are as concerned with their ability to use the Spanish language to function in real life situations. Note also that significant credit is given for effort and creativity.

Included below are optional assessment models that depend on the amount of time available for instruction and the student's level of language proficiency. Multiple alternative assessment models are encouraged.

Optional Model 1:

Optional Model 1 is used with students who generate language on their own or who are comfortable recombining new language and using interlanguage, which has been encouraged throughout the Elements. Use the **Perspectiva** from Element 6 to set the stage for the assessment exercise. Have students develop an album without using the sentence starters. They can use the text as a review for information they choose to include. Use **BLM 6.2** so students can create an original cover using their own art design and text. Also provide students with as many copies of the blank album pages (**BLM 6.3**) as they will need.

Optional Model 2:

Have students work in pairs or small groups to create a "family album." The group might present each area (**familia, amigos, deportes,** etc.) collectively. Brainstorm topics to be included in the album. Use idea mapping for brainstorming. This activity is also conducive to individual artistic expression. Students may draw pictures for the album, or they might design and decorate a group album together. They may also include a tape of their favorite music.

Optional Model 3:

Using a Polaroid camera, create a photo album for the class "family." Encourage students to bring in pictures of their family, activities, and pets. Divide students into cooperative groups. Each group chooses one of the album topics to write about, and is responsible for preparing that one section of the "class family" album. Reserve bulletin board space to present this project.

Optional Model 4:

Prepare a video family or class album. The student's script is the written expression necessary for the assessment. The video presentation illustrates creativity and language use. Students may use the format from the Student Manual to prepare their video album, or they may design their own video album individually, in pairs, in small groups, or as a class.

Optional Model 5:

Using computers and hypermedia, students can prepare an album on disk integrating combinations of text written on the computer, scanned pictures and photos, digitized video, and sound.

ARRIVAL

Picture cards 7a "Airport arrival" and 7b "Immigration counter" may be used with this element.

Contents

1. **Communicative Functions:**

   Imparting and seeking factual information, expressing and finding out intellectual and emotional attitudes, expressing disapproval, getting things done, socializing

2. **Content and Language Skills:**

   Vamos a + infinitive, telling time (24-hour clock), time-zone differences and changes, writing a postcard, customs procedures, greetings and introductions, filling out forms

3. **Culture:**

   Customs procedures, passport control, appropriate gestures and manners when greeting and being introduced to someone

4. **Teaching and Learning Strategies:**

   Role playing, doing mathematical calculations, completing forms

Additional Activity Suggestions (Extension and Interdisciplinary)

1. **Extensions**

   - Get a number of travel itineraries from a local travel agent or airline. Have students practice reading them to obtain key information regarding flight numbers, departure and arrival times, and destinations.

2. **Art/Language Arts**

   - Have students make postcards out of tagboard or poster board. Use the picture side as an art activity. Students may draw or paste on pictures of famous landmarks from a variety of Spanish-speaking countries. Use the message side of the card to have students practice the correct form for writing and addressing a postcard.

3. **Mathematics**

   - Using a time-zone map, have students practice a variety of mathematical calculations.

   - Have students get copies of the latest census information and find out how many or what percentage of Hispanics live in their city, county, and/or state. Have them graph or chart the results.

4. **Social Studies**

   - Ask a representative from a travel agency or government office to talk about the procedures for going through customs when exiting and entering a country.

- Have students get information from a travel agency or government office about legal limits on items that may be taken into other countries.

- Get sample entry/exit duty forms from the airlines and have students practice filling them out.

5. **Advisor/Advisee or Homeroom**

- Discuss and practice the correct form for making introductions.

- Have students go to the library or a local bookstore and obtain a list of books on etiquette. Review and discuss the sections on introductions.

PERSPECTIVA

The **Perspectiva** is an advance organizer intended to stimulate discussion about the topic to be covered in this Element. You may wish to use **BLM 7.0** for this activity. Help students focus on airline travel, flight numbers, cities, and departure and arrival times. Students should also recognize that they will learn how to greet people in Spanish using the appropriate phrases and courtesies.

EXTENSION

Take a field trip to an airport and visit the international terminal. Have students look at the flight departure and arrival boards. Arrange with airport/airline personnel for students to go through a security check point. If possible, arrange for students to visit the inside of an airplane.

VARIATION

BLM 7.0. Using the transparency, help students focus on topics to be covered in this Element. This transparency may also be used for a culminating and/or assessment activity.

A. EL ITINERARIO

Remind students that they will be looking at examples of the schedule and experiences of last year's homestay student, Kristina Sullivan. If your class did not do Element 4, you will need to introduce telling time on the hour and have students make a paper plate clock according to the directions given in that Element.

Ask students if they know the meaning of the title of the activity. Talk about the cognate in English *(itinerary)* and the meaning of the word. Ask them to look at the activity and see if they can find another new word in Spanish that is also a cognate (**practicar**).

Present the phrase ¡**Vamos a practicar!** Introduce the use of the sentence, **Vamos a** + *infinitive* to mean *Let's go do something!* Ask students to think of any of the sports or activities they have learned and put them in a sentence using **Vamos a** _____.

Examples: ¡**Vamos a** + **nadar, jugar al tenis, leer, estudiar!** (Refer to the Personal Information Form in Element 4.)

Discuss the concept of the 24-hour clock. Review the terms **medianoche** and **mediodía**. Remind students of the difference between **Es la una** and the other hours that all begin with **Son las** _____. Then practice on-the-hour time telling with the class. Use any of the techniques suggested in Element 4. Have students use the clocks they made from paper plates in that Element or make new clocks.

NOTA: Present the three expressions used with time at different periods in the day: **por la mañana, de la tarde, de la noche.** These expressions are presented for passive recognition only.

EXTENSION

Game-Password. During class tell students that they will be expected to use the expression **Vamos a** + the infinitive of their choice to exit class. The teacher stands at the door and listens to each student saying the password phrase **Vamos a** + infinitive as he or she leaves the class. Be sure to start this activity well ahead of the time the dismissal bell rings so that all students are required to use a "password phrase" before they can leave the room.

Answer Key:

1:00 P.M.	8:00 P.M.
4:00 P.M.	9:00 P.M.
7:00 P.M.	12:00 A.M.

B. INFORMACIÓN DEL VUELO

Go over the flight information. Draw attention to the use of 13:00. Ask if students remember when they first saw the Spanish expression **llego** *(I'm arriving/I arrive)*. (It was presented in Kristina's letter to the Carmonas in Element 5.) The expression will almost always be **llego a** + **las** and the time of day. The exception, again, will be with 1:00. (**Llego a la una.**) Have students complete the message and address the postcard according to the directions.

EXPANSION

Do a quick review drill using **llego** + a time of day. Use a clock with moveable hands. Show a time and students respond with **llego** + the time shown on your clock. This can be done more quickly by simply going from student to student and having them respond with any time of day they wish.

C. TU RELOJ

In the **Perspectiva** you may have presented the concept of time zones. Ask students to look carefully at the time-zone map. Discuss the concept of time zones and the variations in times. Then have students complete the activity by filling in the blank watch faces according to the directions.

Answer Key:

1. 5:00 A.M.
2. 12:00 P.M.
3. 1:00 P.M.
4. 3:00 A.M.
5. 5:00 A.M.
6. 3:00 P.M.

D. INMIGRACIÓN: CONTROL DE PASAPORTES

Present the terms **inmigración** and **control de pasaportes**. Tell students that this is an example of a typical conversation between a customs official and someone entering a country. Have students read the dialogue quietly to themselves. Clarify the meaning of the Spanish vocabulary. Next, read both parts of the dialogue aloud. Then reread the dialogue, having the class take the role of "you" and respond to the official. Finally, allow time for pair practice. Circulate among students as they are practicing. This is a good time for you to assess their oral proficiency. Prepare a checklist with a ranking from 1–4. As you circulate, give a numerical value to the students' performance. The score can be based on a variety of factors, such as the correct use of phrases, pronunciation, and overall participation in the activity. Note if there are any words or phrases that are causing difficulty. When the practice time is over, review them with the entire group. Do not single out individual problems. Simply state, "These are some of the problem areas I noticed as I was moving around the room." Then make general corrections and allow for group practice. This type of assessment should be used frequently throughout the course.

EXPANSION

Students will need to use the sample passport directions in Element 3.

To practice:

1. Ask for three volunteers to serve as **oficiales de inmigración**.

2. Divide the remaining students into three groups with one checker per group. Each group chooses a country of arrival (examples: México, España, Colombia).

3. **Oficiales de inmigración** prepare for the role play by writing the **oficial de inmigración** part of the conversation on note cards and practicing it quietly.

4. Each group designs a stamp and a sign to represent its chosen country. This will be the customs stamp. The stamp and the sign might reflect something important about the country learned in Element 1 (examples: the flag, national flower, animal).

5. Make several copies/drawings of each stamp.

6. Have groups practice the traveler's part of the conversation.

7. Arrange the room with three **inmigración** tables. Place each sign in front of a table. The **oficiales de inmigración** will sit at the **inmigración** tables.

8. Students from each group file their **inmigración** checkpoint. They use the conversation to gain entry into their chosen country. They may use notes or memorize the traveler's part of the conversation. To enter their homestay country students need to pass the **inmigración** table. For some students it may take a few tries to give the appropriate information.

   Oficiales de inmigración need to have patience. Travelers form their **primera impresión** of a country from the behavior of **oficiales de inmigración**.

9. After a student has given the correct information, the **pasaporte** is stamped with the entry stamp of **inmigración** by the checker. The student may then proceed to the arrival area where the host family is waiting. Begin the **inmigración** process.

E. ¡BIENVENIDO!

Play the tape or read the four dialogue bubbles. Practice the new vocabulary. It is important to use visuals and gestures to convey the meanings of the words and phrases. Gestures also lend authenticity to the language, as well as enhancing students' comprehension. Go over the phrase **estoy un poco cansada** and ask the class how the word for tired will change in Spanish when a male student is talking about himself (cansad**o**).

F. SALUDOS

Present the term **saludos** and review all of the vocabulary from Activity E. Allow time for pair and small-group practice. This is a good activity to use for role playing in front of the class. Remember to ask only for volunteers to perform in front of the class. Use the same technique for assessment that was suggested in Activity D.

VARIATION
BLM 7.1. Using the transparency, students will be able to create written dialogues, which they will practice in groups.

G. PRÁCTICA

This activity moves the focus from listening and speaking to reading and writing. Remember to treat phrases as lexical, not grammatical, items.

Answer Key:

1. c
2. g
3. a
4. e
5. b
6. d
7. f

EXPANSION
BLM 7.2. For additional practice, give each student a card with a ragged line down the center. Tell students to write one of the lines from the airport conversation, putting the Spanish on one half and the English equivalent on the other. Then have students tear each card at the ragged line. Collect and shuffle the cards. Have students match the two halves of a card.

H. MI EQUIPAJE NO ESTÁ

Look at the picture with the class. Ask students to imagine what has happened. Discuss the meaning of the title. Go over the directions and have students complete the form. This activity recycles information from Elements 2, 3, and 4.

I. UNA LLAMADA A LOS ESTADOS UNIDOS

Introduce the vocabulary in the title. If appropriate to the age and developmental level of your class, you can present the difference between the words **a** *(to)* and **de** *(from)*. If a call is coming from the United States, the title would be **Una llamada de los Estados Unidos.** Present the two prepositions as lexical, not grammatical, items. Go over the directions and have students complete the activity.

Answer Key:

1. 9:00 A.M.

2. 5:00 A.M.

3. 10:00 A.M.

4. 9:00 A.M.

The personal information answers will vary.

EXPANSION

BLM 7.3. Copy sufficient Blackline Masters for all the students. They can work individually, in pairs, or in small groups to calculate time-zone conversion. Students must then decide if it is appropriate to call home at that time.

J. MI DIARIO

As students gain more vocabulary, encourage them to use as much Spanish as possible in completing the journal activity. Focus on correct use of words and phrases. Seek gradual error reduction in spelling. Have old magazines and catalogues available to use for pictures. This activity should foster creativity and the opportunity to experiment with new words and phrases. Refer to the **Mi diario** sections in previous Elements for additional suggestions and ideas about using this activity.

8 YOUR HOMESTAY HOUSE AND DAILY ROUTINE

Picture card #8 "Making a snack" may be used with this element.

Contents

1. **Communicative Functions:**

   Imparting and seeking factual information, identifying, reporting (including describing and narrating), asking, socializing

2. **Content and Language Skills:**

   Tengo hambre, rooms of a house, furniture and common household furnishings, expressing daily routine activities with él and yo, telling time before and after the hour

3. **Culture:**

   Comparing snack foods and daily routines

4. **Teaching and Learning Strategies:**

   Listening selectively, using TPR, discerning differences and similarities, organizing, categorizing, interviewing

Additional Activity Suggestions (Extension and Interdisciplinary)

1. **Art or Mechanical Drawing**

   • Draw the floor plan of a house (real or imaginary).

   • Make a bulletin board with the theme of houses. These can be drawn, cut out, or done with a variety of artistic materials. Use a Spanish-English dictionary to add additional vocabulary (roof, walls, door, window, and so on). Once the picture is completed, label it in Spanish.

2. **Language Arts**

   • Write a composition about houses. Compare houses in your region with houses in Spanish-speaking countries.

3. **Social Studies**

   • Go to the library or media center and investigate the concept of "the family."

   • Research the roles of members of Hispanic families using the library or media center and through oral interviews.

   • Compare information on family roles in different cultures, including the nuclear and extended family.

4. **Advisor/Advisee or Homeroom**

   • Have students talk about their families and the roles various members play. Include consideration of single-parent and extended families.

- Have students talk to their grandparents and other older members of the family to find out how family values and roles of family members have changed in the past ten to twenty years.

PERPESPECTIVA

The **Perspectiva** is an advance organizer intended to stimulate discussion about the topics to be covered in the Element. Ask the class to look at the picture. (You may use a transparency of **BLM 8.0**, if you wish.) Through the discussion students should become aware that they will be learning about the house and some of the daily activities of their homestay family.

A. TENGO HAMBRE

Introduce the expression **Tengo hambre**. Review the recipe for making a **nacho**. If possible, bring the actual ingredients to class and use them to introduce the vocabulary.

Students may not have seen the round **tortillas**. These are available in most grocery stores and supermarkets in the dairy section. Try to have both the round **tortilla** and a package of **tortilla** chips as a sample. Explain that there is a difference between **tortillas** made of corn (**de maíz**) and those made of flour (**de harina**). Have a sample of both available.

Using either a single round **tortilla** or a chip, break it into pieces to illustrate **pedazos**.

Talk about the way the directions for recipes are worded. Recipes use commands: put, mix, stir, cook, bake, etc. Ask students to guess the meaning of **pon**; then have them silently read the directions for making the **nacho**. Alert them to the two-step process for reading these directions. Encourage them to guess and infer meaning from the context and also from what they think logically might occur.

VARIATION

Use large pictures or other realia to introduce the vocabulary for the ingredients. Bring the necessary ingredients to class and assemble a **nacho**. Teach the directions by doing TPR. If you do not have access to a kitchen area such as the home economics classroom, use a microwave oven in your classroom.

EXTENSION

Here is another **salsa** recipe that you might try with your class. It is also known as **Pico de Gallo** or **Salsa Fresca**. This recipe shows students a different kind of **salsa**. Explain that there are various kinds of **salsas**.

Salsa Fresca

4 medium tomatoes / **4 tomates medianos**
1 small onion finely chopped / **1 cebolla cortada**
2–3 jalapeños or serrano peppers stemmed, seeded, and chopped / **2–3 jalapeños o serranos sin semillas y cortados**
1/4 cup cilantro / **1/4 taza cilantro**
1 small clove garlic, minced / **1 oreja de ajo, cortado**

2 tablespoons lime juice / **2 cucharadas de jugo de limón**
salt / **sal**
ground pepper / **pimienta**

Cut tomatoes in half; remove seeds. Coarsely chop tomatoes. Combine tomatoes, onion, jalapeños, cilantro, garlic, and lime juice in medium bowl. Add salt and black pepper to taste. Cover and refrigerate one hour or up to three days for flavors to blend. Makes 2 1/2 cups.

EXTENSION

Table Setting. Learning the Spanish words for drinking glass, cup, plate, napkin, knife, fork, and spoon is useful for students. Bring the items to class and use them as visuals to teach the vocabulary. Hold up each item and identify it using the Spanish name. For example, **Esto es un vaso** *(This is a drinking glass)*. Then put the drinking glass on the table while saying, **Estoy poniendo el vaso en la mesa** *(I'm putting the glass on the table)*. Follow the same procedure with the other objects. As a next step, repeat the phrase identifying the object and then hand it to a student while saying, for example **Toma el vaso** *(Take the glass)*. Then give the TPR command, **Pon el vaso en la mesa** *(Put the glass on the table)*. Continue this procedure with all of the objects. Allow ample time for language input. When students are comfortable with the vocabulary, you may wish to have them say what they are doing while using the sentence, **Estoy poniendo** *(name of object)* **en la mesa**. Extend the activity by giving a variety of commands asking students to do different things with the objects, such as giving one to another student.

VARIATION

You may wish to have students use the table-setting objects from **BLM 8.1** for any of these suggested table-setting activities.

EXPANSION

TPR. Have available sufficient quantities of the above items in paper or plastic. You may wish to have a variety of sizes of plates, glasses, and cups. If it is age and developmentally appropriate, use them to teach **grande** *(large)* and **pequeño/a** *(small)*. Each student should have one to five of each of the items on his or her desk. Teach the term **la mesa** *(table)*. Using the command **Pon**, that they learned in the recipe for **nacho**, give a variety of TPR commands using the table-setting vocabulary. Examples: **Pon el vaso en la mesa. Pon el plato sobre el vaso.** When students are comfortable with the vocabulary, ask them to put different numbers of objects on the table. Examples: **Pon dos vasos en la mesa. Pon tres tazas sobre dos platos.**

EXPANSION

TPR review of colors and numbers. Have available the quantities of the paper or plastic items in a variety of colors learned in Element 2. Give a variety of commands using the name of the objects along with a specified number and/or color.

EXPANSION

Table Setting. (BLM 8.1) There are a variety of activities that can be done with this Blackline Master. Duplicate sufficient quantities of the master for each student to have a least one. For some of the suggested activities, you may wish to give each student several copies.

First, have students cut out the drinking glass, cup, and silverware items and label them in Spanish. Have them cut circles out of paper for plates and use a folded sheet of paper as a napkin.

SUGGESTED ACTIVITIES:

1. Have students label and color the table-setting objects. Use these paper objects they have colored to do the activities as suggested.

2. Have students work in pairs giving TPR commands to each other using the table-setting objects.

3. Game: What's Missing?

   • Give each student an envelope large enough to contain the objects. Students can use only the paper silverware objects in a smaller envelope or all of the objects in a larger brown envelope.

   • Teach the question, Do you have a *name of object?* (¿Tienes un/una *name of object in Spanish?*)

   • Students work in pairs. Each student begins with all of the objects in his or her envelope. Student A removes one of the objects from his or her envelope and hides it. Student B tries to guess which object is missing by asking the question **¿Tienes un _____?** Student A responds **sí** or **no**. The guessing continues until Student B discovers which object is missing from the envelope. Then students switch roles.

B. LOS CUARTOS DE LA CASA

Ask students to look at the picture as you identify each of the rooms of the house using the Spanish name. Model the names a second time and have students repeat them after you. Present the phrase **Aquí está** *(Here is)*. Then proceed with the activity.

Teacher Script

Read the following sentences as a tour script and watch as students point to the room in the picture in the text. Read in any order you like. Read the tour several times in a different order. Walk around as you do to check that students are correctly identifying each room.

1. Aquí está el dormitorio.

2. Aquí está el cuarto de baño.

3. Aquí está la sala.

4. Aquí está la cocina.

5. Aquí está el comedor.

   Allow time for students to work in pairs. Student A identifies a room and Student B points to that room in the picture. Then students switch roles. Each may name one or more of the rooms at a time.

EXPANSION

Create a house floor plan in the classroom. Use masking tape or string on the floor to indicate the rooms. Have students label the rooms in Spanish and decorate them with pictures or actual furniture and other household items.

C. LOS MUEBLES Y OTRAS COSAS DE LA CASA

Remind the students of the use of **el** and **la** meaning *the*. Go through the items, introducing the vocabulary to students. Have them repeat the words in Spanish. Once students are familiar with the vocabulary, allow time for the ¡**Vamos a practicar!** activity. Walk around the room while students are working in pairs to confirm that they are correctly identifying the items.

EXTENSION

Categorizando. Tell students the name of the next activity is **Categorizando** and have them guess the meaning of this title. If it is age and developmentally appropriate, tell them that the Spanish ending **-ando** or **-iendo** of a word is equivalent to the English ending *-ing*. Next, have students write the names of five rooms as headings on a piece of paper. Then ask them to categorize the words for furniture and appliances according to the rooms in which they belong. Allow ample time for them to complete the lists. Encourage them to make a separate list of any of these items that might be found in more than one room of the house (example: lamp, chair, radio, television).

EXTENSION

Interdisciplinary Activity/Art. Have students draw a picture of their own room or of their "ideal" room. Tell them to draw and decorate the room, then label it in Spanish. Let them talk about their pictures to a small group of classmates. Put the pictures on a bulletin board.

D. ¡PON LOS MUEBLES EN LOS CUARTOS! (BLM 8.2)

EXPANSION

TPR Activity. Use the floor plan in the student book on page 87 for this activity. Duplicate sufficient copies of the Blackline Master to have one for each student.

Other supplies:

- Old magazines and catalogues from which students may cut pictures

- Scissors, tape, paste or glue

- Drawing paper, crayons, pencils, and markers

Be sure that each student has a picture or drawing of each of the pieces of furniture and other household items. You may wish to put the following checklist on the chalkboard:

la bañera

la cama

la cocina de gas

la ducha

el escritorio

el lavabo

la lámpara

la mesa

la radio

el refrigerador

la silla

el sillón

el sofá

la televisión

la toalla

Review the command **pon** *(put)*. Read the script at a normal speaking pace. Walk around the room as you read the script. Watch to see if students are correctly placing the items in the appropriate room.

Teacher Script:

1. Pon la radio en el dormitorio.
2. Pon la cama en el dormitorio.
3. Pon la lampara en el dormitorio.
4. Pon el sofá en la sala.
5. Pon el lavabo en el cuarto de baño.
6. Pon la mesa en el comedor.
7. Pon el refrigerador en la cocina.
8. Pon la cocina de gas en la cocina.
9. Pon la bañera en el cuarto de baño.
10. Pon el escritorio en el dormitorio.
11. Pon la toalla en el cuarto de baño.
12. Pon la televisión en la sala.
13. Pon la mesa en la cocina.
14. Pon la lámpara en la sala.
15. Pon la ducha en el cuarto de baño.

VARIATION

Vary the above script with responses that are illogical, but fun! Example: **Pon el refrigerador en el cuarto de baño.**

E. UN DÍA CON ALEJANDRO

Tell students that they are going to learn how to talk about some common daily activities using the Spanish expressions. Say that you are going to describe what Alejandro is doing in each of the pictures. Go through the series of pictures, saying the sentences in Spanish. Go through the series a second time and have students repeat the sentences.

¡Vamos a practicar!

Have students complete the matching activity.

Answer Key:

1. e

2. d

3. g

4. h

5. i

6. a

7. b

8. c

9. f

EXPANSION

Un día con Alejandro. (BLM 8.3, 8.4, 8.5) Make sufficient copies of each of the Blackline Masters for every student. Have students cut them into individual pictures, for a total of nine; spread the pictures on their desk, arranging the activities in the daily schedule routine sequence; and write the activity in Spanish on the reverse side of the picture.

Move around the room slowly as you describe each of the daily activities. Ask students to hold up the picture that corresponds to that activity. Allow a minimum of eight seconds for students to process the sentences they hear. Monitor student responses as you walk around the room.

F. ¿CUÁNDO?

Before students look at the activity in their books, do the following oral preparation: Review the numbers from 1 to 30. Introduce the interrogative ¿cuándo? *(when?)*. Review telling time (on the hour). To do so, use a clock with moveable hands, draw clocks, or write times on the chalkboard. Using this same technique, introduce the concept of telling time after the hour and before the hour. Illustrate the time on the clock face as you say it in Spanish. Introduce y **cuarto**, **menos cuarto**, and y **media** last.

After this preparation, go through the information at the beginning of Activity G with the class. Read the times indicated on the clock faces in the second part of the activity as a response to the question ¿cuándo? After students have practiced using these additional expressions for telling time, have them fill in the blanks using the new expressions.

Answer Key:

1. nueve

2. menos

3. menos cuarto

4. y

5. y cuarto

6. y media

G. EL HORARIO DE ALEJANDRO

Introduce the activity and review the directions with students. Read the following sentences. As you read the times, students should write the numerals (indicated in parentheses) in the blanks in their books.

Teacher Script

Example: Alejandro se levanta a las siete y cuarto. (7:15)

1. Alejandro desayuna a las ocho menos diez. (7:50)

2. Alejandro va a la escuela a las nueve. (9:00)

3. Alejandro almuerza a las doce y media. (12:30)

4. Alejandro hace su tarea a las seis menos veinte. (5:40)

5. Alejandro juega con sus amigos a las siete y veinte. (7:20)

6. Alejandro cena a las diez menos cuarto. (9:45)

7. Alejandro mira la televisión a las tres y diez. (3:10)

8. Alejandro se acuesta a las diez y vienticinco. (10:25)

Read the sentences again and have students call out the times of day in English to verify their answers. Then allow time for them to read the sentences with a partner. Walk around the room while they are reading the sentences to listen for possible high-frequency problem areas in pronunciation and conceptualization of telling time.

VARIATION

Have students reread the sentences in pairs, changing the times of day.

EXPANSION

For additional writing practice, you may wish to have students write the times of day in words instead of numerals.

H. TU HORARIO

This activity introduces the yo forms of the expressions in Activity F. Present them as lexical items, not as grammatical or verb forms. Tell students that you will model the sentences the way they will use them when referring to themselves. Read each sentence once. Model the sentences a second time and have students repeat them.

The second part of the activity involves writing. Go through the directions with the class. Be sure students are familiar with the expressions they need to use. Tell them that they may select any time of day they wish; however, they should be logical in terms of what time they might actually do the various activities. Allow ample time for them to complete the sentences.

Answer Key:

The time of day indicated in each sentence will vary. If students use 1:00, check to be sure that they have changed **a las** to **a la.**

1. Yo me levanto a las 6:15.

2. Yo desayuno a las _____.

3. Yo voy a la escuela a las _____.

4. Yo almuerzo a las _____.

5. Yo juego con mis amigos a las _____.

6. Yo hago mi tarea a las _____.

7. Yo miro la televisión a las _____.

8. Yo ceno a las _____.

9. Yo me acuesto a las _____.

EXPANSION

Dictation/Cultural Comparison. Semejanzas y diferencias: Comparación de horarios. (BLM 8.6) This is a two-part expansion activity. It is designed to have students 1) practice writing from dictation and 2) think about the cultural differences that may exist by comparing the times of day when certain activities take place.

Duplicate enough copies of the Blackline Master for each student. Go over the directions with the class.

a) Listening/Dictation Exercise

Students listen as you dictate the Spanish phrase for each of the activities. They write the Spanish for the activity in the blank. The time is already written for them. Read the sentences at a moderately normal pace. Read the entire sentence once. Tell students to listen only during this first reading. Read the sentence a second time. Students complete the sentences by filling in the blanks in the column labeled **Alejandro.**

Teacher Script/Answer Key: (Students write the underlined portion.)

1. Se levanta a las siete.

2. Desayuna a las ocho.

3. Va a la escuela a las nueve.

4. Almuerza en la casa a las doce y media.

5. Hace su tarea a las seis y media antes de la cena.

6. Juega con sus amigos a las siete y media.

7. Cena tarde. Cena a las ocho.

8. Mira la televisión a las nueve.

9. Se acuesta a la una de la manaña.

Have students check their dictation by referring to the sentences in their book. You may also wish to put the correct responses on the chalkboard or an overhead transparency. This may be done as a pair activity.

b) Comparison

Have students go back and fill in the column headed **Yo** with the time of day they normally do the activity. After the activity is completed, conduct a discussion about the differences in schedules.

EXPANSION

Cultural comparison. Discuss the following information with students:

One of the most obvious differences in daily schedules is in the meal times. Breakfast times vary according to when the work day begins, but generally include coffee with milk (**café con leche**) or hot chocolate and bread. Lunch is the main meal of the day. It is eaten in most of Spanish America during a late noon hour. Many Spanish-speaking people have a snack (**una merienda**) in the late afternoon or early evening. Supper is a light meal and is eaten late in the evening. In some Spanish-speaking countries, this may be as late as 10:00 P.M. to 11:00 P.M.

I. UNA ENTREVISTA CON TUS AMIGOS

Discuss the directions for the activity with students. Remind them that they have done surveys (**encuestas**) in previous Elements. The interview (**entrevista**) is designed to have them talk to at least two of their friends about their daily schedules and compare the differences and similarities. Answers will vary.

J. MI DIARIO

As students continue to increase their ability to use more Spanish vocabulary, encourage them to incorporate as much of this as possible in completing the journal activity. Emphasize the correct use of words and phrases over exact accuracy in spelling or pronunciation. Seek gradual error reduction, not complete and immediate error elimination.

Have old magazines and catalogues available to use for pictures. If some students are artistically inclined, encourage them to draw pictures instead of cutting them out. The **diario** activity should foster creativity and the opportunity to experiment with new words and phrases. It is designed to be an individual effort, permitting the maximum expression of each student's linguistic and well as other talents and abilities. If you are using the **diario** as an instrument for assessment, be certain that students understand exactly how their work will be evaluated. You may wish to refer to the **Mi diario** sections in previous Elements for additional suggestions and ideas about using this activity.

GETTING AROUND TOWN

Picture cards 9a "In the park", 9b "Outside post office", and 9c "At the café" may be used with this element.

Contents

1. **Communicative Functions:**

   Seeking factual information (identifying, asking), asking and following directions, finding out intellectual attitudes (offering to do something, expressing/inquiring about obligation to do something), expressing and finding out emotional attitudes (expressing preference, likes/dislikes, intention, want/desire), expressing appreciation, socializing

2. **Content and Language Skills:**

   Directions (**a la derecha, a la izquierda, sigue derecho**); prepositional phrases of position (**en frente de, detras de, al lado de**); common city/town buildings, and places; expressions of personal need (**tengo hambre, tengo sed, estoy enfermo(a), me perdí**)

3. **Culture:**

   Arrangement of cities and towns, where to find necessities (stamps, money exchange, etc.), reading local/international signs, ethnic foods and dietary differences

4. **Teaching and Learning Strategies:**

   Listening selectively, using TPR, organizing, discerning differences and similarities, categorizing, interviewing

Additional Activity Suggestions (Extension and Interdisciplinary)

1. **Extension**

   • Take students on a field trip to a restaurant that serves Spanish ethnic foods.

2. **Social Studies**

   • Have students research and discuss the historical/social significance of mealtimes in various cultures.

3. **Art**

   • Study and discuss differences in architectural styles (churches/public buildings).

   • Make a poster or collage of famous buildings in a Spanish-speaking country.

4. **Mechanical Drawing**

   • Design a drawing or plan for a town or city with important buildings.

5. **Language Arts**

- Do a webbing activity with buildings as a theme. Select a topic for a written or oral report.

6. **Home Economics**

- Prepare some typical ethnic foods. (See Element 8.)

- Collect menus from a number of area restaurants and see how many foreign food names appear on them.

- Investigate what constitutes a well-balanced diet. Do a report on basic food groups.

- Do a webbing activity with foods as a theme.

7. **Advisor/Advisee or Homeroom**

Discuss the role of food in U.S. society. What role does fast food play in our daily lives?

PERSPECTIVA

The **Perspectiva** is an advance organizer intended to stimulate discussion about the topics to be covered in this Element. (You may wish to use **BLM 9.0** for this discussion.) This **Perspectiva** presents the two major themes of getting around town and reading a restaurant menu.

Tell students to look at the half page of various city and building signs. Ask them why these would be important signs to someone visiting a new city. Discuss under what circumstances you might need or want to find any of these places.

Review the short menu with students. Focus on the major menu divisions of appetizers, soups and salads, entrees, desserts, and beverages. Tell students that they will have an opportunity to learn about some foods that commonly appear on menus in Spanish-speaking countries.

A. LAS SEÑALES DE LA CIUDAD (BLM 9.1)

Activity A further develops the theme presented in the first part of the **Perspectiva**. Review the signs with the class. Be sure that students understand the meanings of the signs. Then go over the Spanish pronunciation. Present the words and have students repeat them. When they are comfortable with the meaning and pronunciation, go through the list of things to do and help them correlate the task to be accomplished with the appropriate sign. Read each of the tasks and ask students to tell you the Spanish sign that would correlate to that task. Ask for individual volunteers or whole-group response.

Answer Key:

1. banco

2. correo

3. Calle Simón Bolívar

4. Palacio de las Bellas Artes

5. parque

6. damas/caballeros

7. Catedral de San Juan de la Cruz

8. teléfono

9. cine

10. estación del tren

Duplicate enough copies of the **BLM 9.1** for each student. Allow time for students to paste the appropriate sign onto the corresponding sentence in their book.

B. FRASES CLAVES (BLM 9.2 AND BLM 9.3)

Before beginning the activity in the student book, introduce the ten phrases. You may do this in one of two ways:

1. Make an overhead transparency of both Blackline Masters. Show only the picture relating to the phrase you are presenting. Cover the other four pictures with plain paper to avoid confusion. Model the phrase in Spanish as you show the picture. Have students repeat after you.

2. Make a copy of the Blackline Masters and cut each sheet into separate strips. You may wish to enlarge the pictures on the copy machine. Hold up the appropriate picture as you introduce each phrase. Have students repeat after you.

Direct students to the phrases written in their book. Read the phrases in Spanish and have students read each one after you. Allow time for a pair activity. Have pairs work together to guess the English meaning of each phrase. Tell them they may refer to the pictures and cognates for help. Verify the responses with the class. Then allow time for students to write the English meaning of each phrase on the appropriate line in their text. Check their answers.

EXTENSION

Duplicate enough copies of both Blackline Masters for students. Tell students to look at the pictures on the cards and decide which of the phrases they would use to respond to each situation. Tell them to write the phrase they choose on the back of each picture. Circulate around the room while they are writing and verify the answers with the class. You can do this by:

• using the overhead and writing or saying the phrase while showing the picture

• writing the responses on the board

Encourage oral repetition of the phrases in association with the picture. Have students work in pairs. One holds up the cards while the other responds to them.

EXPANSION

When students have practiced using these phrases, have them work in small groups or teams to write out or draw other situations in which these **frases claves** can be of use. When each team has completed creating new situations, they can ask another team to play the review game.

C. DIRECCIONES

This activity teaches three Spanish phrases needed to follow directions:

dobla a la derecha	turn right
dobla a la izquierda	turn left
sigue derecho (en)	go straight (on)

Also present **pasa** *(pass, go past)* and **está** *(is, it is)* before beginning the directions. These two terms are not in the student book. The activity also presents three prepositional phrases of location that are useful when following directions:

en frente de	in front of
detrás de	behind
al lado de	next to, beside

If it is age and developmentally appropriate, you may wish to tell students that **de** is used after each of the expressions. With the exception of **en frente de**, **de** does not have an English equivalent.

Have students look at the drawings illustrating the directions and locations. Then model the phrases by TPR and demonstration. Use a clear acetate on the overhead to demonstrate the phrases. Practice the phrases with students. When you are sure that they are comfortable with the meanings, give them time for pair practice. Partner A gives the direction and Partner B does the action.

The prepositional phrases can be demonstrated using any object(s) and a small box, such as a shoebox. Place the object in each of the three positions. You may also wish to add the prepositional phrase **dentro (de)**, *inside*. In pair practice, allow students to select their own objects for demonstration. This is a good opportunity to recycle vocabulary (items of clothing, household furnishings, table-setting items, etc. from the Blackline Masters from previous Elements).

D. EL MAPA

Read the directions slowly. Make sure that students have enough time to process the language and follow the directions. Tell students to put their pencil on A, **Mi casa,** to start.

Teacher Script:

1. Dobla a la izquierda.

    Sigue derecho en la Avenida de la Independencia hasta la Avenida de las Bellas Artes.

    Dobla a la derecha.

    Sigue derecho en la Avenida de las Bellas Artes hasta la Calle Simón Bolívar.

    Dobla a la izquierda.

    Al lado izquierda está el banco.

They should arrive at building G. Verify the location. Repeat the directions, if necessary. Have students write **el banco** in G.

E. ¡PRACTICAMOS LAS DIRECCIONES!

Here are several additional sets of directions to read to students. Each time they should arrive at a different location. Read the directions slowly. Make sure they have enough time to process the language. Tell students to put their pencil on A, **Mi casa,** to start.

Teacher Scripts:

1. Dobla a la derecha.

   Sigue derecho en la Avenida de la Independencia hasta la Calle Greco.

   Dobla a la izquierda.

   Sigue derecho en la Calle Greco hasta la Avenida de las Américas.

   Dobla a la izquierda.

   Pasa la Calle 5 de Mayo.

   El correo está a la derecha.

They should arrive at building E. Verify the location. Repeat the directions, if necessary. Have students write **el correo** in E.

2. Dobla a la izquierda.

   Sigue en la Avenida de la Independencia hasta la Calle Cervantes.

   Dobla a la izquierda.

   El hospital está a la derecha.

They should arrive at building B. Verify the location. Repeat the directions, if necessary. Have students write **el hospital** in B.

3. Dobla a la derecha.

   Sigue en la Avenida de la Independencia hasta la Calle Greco.

   Dobla a la izquierda.

   Sigue en la Calle Greco hasta la Calle Simón Bolívar.

   Dobla a la izquierda.

   El cine está a la izquierda.

They should arrive at building D. Verify the location. Repeat the directions, if necessary. Have students write **el cine** in D.

4. Dobla a la izquierda.

   Sigue en la Avenida de la Independencia hasta la Avenida Diego Rivera.

   Dobla a la derecha.

   El parque está a la izquierda.

They should arrive at location H. Verify the location. Repeat the directions, if necessary. Have students write **el parque** in H.

EXPANSION

Not all of the streets and buildings/locations are used in the above scripts. You are strongly urged to create your own scripts for them. You may also wish to have students create different scripts and read them to a partner, in small groups, or to the entire class.

Answer Key:

A. mi casa

B. el hospital

C. la estación del tren

D. el cine

E. el correo

F. la catedral

G. el banco

H. el parque

F. LA PLAZA

This activity can take several days. You may wish to have students do it concurrently with other activities. As you present the list, do some preliminary identification of each of the persons mentioned. Mention that the individual was, for example, a writer, an artist, or a discoverer (a basic identification follows). Arrange for the class to use the library or media center to do the research. Depending on the age and developmental level of students, this activity may be assigned as a small-group or an independent project.

1. Francisco Franco (Spanish government official)

2. Gabriela Mistral (Chilean author/poet)

3. El Greco (Domenicos Theotocopoulos) (Spanish artist)

4. Simón Bolívar (South American liberator/freedom fighter)

5. Porfirio Díaz (Mexican government official)

6. Moctezuma (Aztec leader)

7. Joan Miró (Spanish artist)

8. Francisco de Goya (Spanish artist)

9. Hernán Cortés (Spanish explorer)

10. El Rey Juan Carlos (King of Spain)

11. Benito Juárez (Mexican freedom fighter)

12. José Martí (Cuban author/poet)

13. Ponce de León (Spanish explorer)

14. Francisco de Coronado (Spanish explorer)

15. Diego Velázquez (Spanish artist)

16. Gabriel García Márquez (Colombian author)

17. Miguel de Cervantes (Spanish author)

18. Salvador Dalí (Spanish artist)

Review the information requested on the research card. When students have completed their research, have them fill in the cards. Provide time for reporting and sharing of information.

INTERDISCIPLINARY EXPANSION

Language Arts. Have students complete and present reports with extended information on their selection. They may wish to present pictures of the person and places associated with them. If the famous person is an author, have the student talk about the author's writing or read some of it in translation. Students may also research the availability of videos about the authors or examples of their works.

Art: If the famous person is an artist, have the student prepare a bulletin board showing some of the artist's work.

G. UNA ESTATUA DE UNA PERSONA FAMOSA

Have students draw or paste a picture of the person they selected in Activity F. They may wish to draw a statue of the person. Encourage them to be creative in the way they visually represent their choice. They can also use photocopies of pictures from resource books. They should use their research card to complete the plaque below the picture.

H. EL CORREO

Bring the actual items or realia into class to introduce the vocabulary. Other expressions should be presented visually whenever possible. Use TPR, pictures, and pantomime to introduce them. Go over the phrases, modeling them several times in Spanish. Have students repeat them.

Set up a series of situations like the one presented in the student book. In each case, ask for volunteers to give the responses. Two examples follow:

You walk into the post office. How do you greet the young woman at the window?

Response: Buenos días, Señorita.

You want to send an airmail letter. What do you say?

Response: Quiero enviar un aerograma.

Guide students into writing as well as speaking with this activity. Allow time for them to prepare the dialogue as suggested in their book. Encourage them to develop additional dialogues by combining words and phrases from the various columns. Circulate among students as they are working. Check for correct use of the vocabulary. Encourage correct pronunciation, but do not overemphasize this aspect of the activity. Ask for volunteers to present their dialogues to the class. Provide "props" such as postcards, stamps, and a postal employee hat or badge.

EXPANSION

Writing Activity.

- Give the sentences and phrases as dictation. Avoid using isolated vocabulary words. Allow students to correct their work individually or with a partner.

- Set the situation in English and ask students to write the phrase or sentence they would use. Example: You walk into the post office. How do you greet the young woman at the window? They write: **Buenos días, Señorita.** Allow students to correct their work individually or with a partner.

I. UNA TARJETA POSTAL

In this activity, students practice writing and addressing postcards to friends and family in the United States. This is an opportunity for students to be creative with the written language. Encourage them to use words and phrases they have learned. Focus on authentic and appropriate use of the language (vocabulary). Syntax and grammatical structure are secondary. Seek gradual error elimination in grammar and syntax. Do not insist on precise spelling or complete sentence structure.

EXPANSION

Writing Activity and Interdisciplinary — Art. (BLM 9.4) Duplicate enough of the Blackline Master for each student to have one or more cards. These additional cards may be used for further practice in writing. Encourage students who wish to do so to draw or paste pictures on the reverse side of the cards. The picture may be a place that they might have visited during their homestay. It can also be related to the famous person they selected for their research card. Encourage artistic creativity! NOTE: You may wish to duplicate these on card-stock. Laminate the students' cards when they are finished. This is an excellent "report card" to send home.

J. EL MENÚ

Review the menu with students. Tell them to look for cognates and to guess the meanings of the items in Spanish. Practice the pronunciation of the vocabulary in Spanish. Included below are English translations for items on the menu.

El menú/*Menu*

Entremeses/*Appetizers*

Plátanos fritos/*fried bananas*

Calamares fritos/*fried squid*

Ensaladas y sopas/*Salads and soups*

Ensalada mixta (tomate, lechuga, cebolla)/*tossed salad (tomato, lettuce, onion)*

Ensalada de tomate/*tomato salad*

Guacamole/*salad of mashed avocado mixed with lime, tomato, and garlic*

Consomé con limón/*chicken broth flavored with lemon juice*

Sopa de mariscos/*seafood soup*

Sopa del día/*soup of the day*

Platos principales/*Entrees*

Pollo frito/*fried chicken*

Carne de res con ajo/*beef with garlic*

Paella Valenciana/*chicken with saffron-flavored rice and mixed seafood (clams, shrimp)*

Bistec/*roast beef*

Empanadas de pollo/*chicken, potato, and vegetables wrapped in crust*

Lechón asado/*roast pork*

Salmón a la parrillada/*grilled salmon*

Mariscos fritos/*fried seafood*

Postres/*Desserts*

Torta de fresas/*strawberry cake*

Flan/*custard*

Galletas/*cookies*

Torta de chocolate/*chocolate cake*

Helado (vainilla, fresa, chocolate)/*ice cream (vanilla, strawberry, chocolate)*

Bebidas/*Beverages*

Coca cola, limonada, naranja, agua mineral/*Coke, lemonade, orange, mineral water*

Café, té/*coffee, tea*

Jugo de naranja, guava, papaya, piña/*orange, guava, papaya, pineapple juice*

VARIATION

Bring in actual menu items and/or present the vocabulary using pictures or realia such as plastic and/or paper.

EXPANSION

Have magazines, catalogues, and drawing supplies available. Students can make flash cards of the various menu items by pasting pictures on 3 X 5 index cards. Larger flash cards can be made using shirt cardboard. These flash cards can be used for practice in Activity K. The smaller cards can be placed in the word box/bank, as suggested in Element 1.

When students are comfortable with the vocabulary, have them categorize the foods in the columns. Remind them that some of the foods have special seasonings or are mixed with other foods; however, they should be categorized according to the main ingredient. Verify the responses with the class as a group.

After completing the categories, students should select their dinner items and circle them on the menu in their book.

VARIATIONS

- Verify the responses by having volunteers read their answers.

- Put the categories on a blank overhead. Show the transparency when all students have completed the exercise.

- Have a student(s) do the activity on a blank transparency or a large piece of paper and show it to the class.

K. ¿EN QUÉ PUEDO SERVIRLE?

Introduce the term for *waiter/waitress*. Present the two sentences. Model each one several times in Spanish and have students repeat after you. Allow time for pair practice. If students have made flash cards, have them use these for this activity.

L. JUEGO DE LA CIUDAD

BLM 9.5 and BLM 9.6. Duplicate enough copies of the Blackline Master game board and make several copies of the playing cards for each group. Review the directions with students. The object of the game is to reach the **Casa de helados** *(Ice cream parlor/store)* with as few cards as possible. Go over the additional phrases and be sure all of the students understand them. Then continue:

- Divide the class into teams of two to four players to play this traveler's game.

- Give each team a stack of cards.

- Give one die per group and a colored token for each player.

NOTE: Not all items on the game board have corresponding cards. Also, some cards are subject to different interpretations.

Proceed with the game. Circulate among students to answer questions and to be sure they understand the process. You may wish to have prizes for the winners. It may be helpful to play the game several times over a period of a week. Have students keep track of the winners and give a prize to the person with the most "wins."

EXPANSION

TPR Game, The Living City. (BLM 9.7, 9.8) Use **BLM 9.7** and **BLM 9.8** for this activity. **BLM 9.7** contains pictures of city places with the name of the location in Spanish. **BLM 9.8** contains the situation cards. **NOTE:** If possible, photocopy the cards on cardstock and laminate in order to save them.

Divide students into two teams. Students on both teams are each given a picture from **BLM 9.7**.

Always begin with one student representing a building or location in place. Then:

1. Read the situation card (**BLM 9.8**) to the entire class.

2. Students from each team arrange themselves according to the directions given on the situation card.

3. Verify their arrangement for comprehension.

4. Repeat with another situation card.

The following is a translation of each of the situation cards 1–4.

Situation 1

Next to the bank is the Palace of Fine Arts. To the left of the bank is the train station. In front of the bank is the school. Behind this school are the bathrooms/restrooms. The post office is behind the Palace of Fine Arts.

Situation 2

The train station is in front of the post office. In front of the train station are the bathrooms/restrooms. To the left of the train station is the Palace of Fine Arts. The bank is next to the train station.

Situation 3

The train station is in front of the bank. Next to the bank is the Palace of Fine Arts. Behind the Palace of Fine Arts is the school. To the left of the school is the post office. The bathrooms/restrooms are to the right of the school.

Situation 4

The school is to the right of the Palace of Fine Arts. In front of the school is the post office. To the right of the school is the bank. To the right of this bank are the bathrooms/restrooms. The train station is behind the bathrooms.

VARIATION

Have a student volunteer read the directions.

VARIATION

Small-group activity. Divide the class into groups. There should be as many members as there are buildings or locations in the situation. Select a leader to read the directions to the team. The leader may coach those group members who do not understand the directions the first time they are given. After the directions are given, the leader verifies the arrangement of the group members.

VARIATION

Team competition. This activity is the same as the original, except the teams compete. Have two teams listen as the situation is read. The team that can get in the right order first wins.

VARIATION

Make up your own situation cards or have students work in groups to create new situations.

M. MI DIARIO

Although the famous person information will be in English, encourage students to use as much Spanish as possible in this culminating activity. Refer to the **Mi diario** section in Element 8 for additional suggestions. There are also a number of suggestions in this same section of previous Elements.

10 GOING TO SCHOOL IN YOUR HOMESTAY COUNTRY

Picture cards 10a "Club schedule" and 10b "School supplies" may be used with this element.

Contents

1. **Communicative Functions:**

   Imparting and seeking factual information (reporting and asking), expressing and finding out emotional attitudes (liking and disliking), expressing preferences

2. **Content and Language Skills:**

   School subjects and extracurricular activities, school supplies, presenting a project, self-evaluation and assessment

3. **Culture:**

   Similarities and differences in schools (school subjects, schedules, and extracurricular activities and sports)

4. **Teaching and Learning Strategies:**

   Listening selectively, establishing preferences, predicting, doing puzzles, playing games, polling, brainstorming, labeling, organizing and presenting a project, summarizing

Additional Activity Suggestions (Extension and Interdisciplinary)

1. **Art**

   - Have students do a collage representing school subjects and supplies.

2. **Mathematics**

   - Set up a mock bookstore (**librería**) or stationery and paper supply store (**papelería**). Give students play money and have them go to the store and purchase the items they need. Students can play the roles of store employee and buyer.

3. **Advisor/Advisee or Homeroom**

   - Discuss the process of selecting classes and extracurricular activities. Talk about the appropriate reasons for making these choices.

   - Invite a counselor to talk to students about scheduling classes. It may be helpful for students to understand how classes are scheduled for the entire school.

PERSPECTIVA

The **Perspectiva** is intended to be an advance organizer to stimulate discussion about the topic to be covered in this Element. (You may wish to use BLM 10.0 for this discussion.) This Element presents school subjects and clubs or extracurricular activities. Explain that they will learn the Spanish names for subjects and activities. Alert students that they will also be preparing a project about their school.

A. LAS MATERIAS

Introduce the term **las materias** *(school subjects)*. Ask students to look at the list and follow as you pronounce the Spanish terms. You may wish to take this opportunity to do a quick review of the masculine and feminine singular forms of *the* in Spanish: **el (los)** and **la (las)**. Review the forms as lexical items all meaning *the*. Do not emphasize the grammatical concept. Practice the pronunciation of the vocabulary with students. Allow time for them to write the English equivalents on the lines provided.

EXPANSION

Flash cards. Using 3 X 5 index cards, have students cut out or draw pictures depicting each of the school subjects and place them it on the cards. Some examples are a musical note (**la música**), a globe (**la geografía**), and a math formula (**las matemáticas**). Have students write the corresponding Spanish term on the reverse side of the card. Allow time for pair work to practice the vocabulary. These cards also may be used to practice the sentences introduced in Activity G. The cards can be placed in the individual student's word bank started in earlier Elements.

B. LOS CLUBES

Follow the same procedure as Activity A to introduce the vocabulary. Go through the list with students and have them circle any of the activities that they also have in their school. Remind them that the words **el, la, los,** and **las** *(the)* are used with the names of the school subjects and clubs, but we do not express *the* in English. (**Las** does not appear in this activity.) Allow time for students to write the English equivalents in the blanks. Verify the answers with the class.

EXPANSION

Flash cards. Follow the same procedure as Activity A. Example: camera (**la fotografía**), bicycle (**el cyclismo**), thespian masks (**el drama**).

Review the **NOTA** with the class. Encourage students to be curious about the phenomenon of language, and talk to them about the origin of words.

EXTENSION

Have the students consult a comprehensive dictionary for the origin of English words.

C. MIS PREFERENCIAS

Review the registration form with the class. This form recycles vocabulary that was introduced in completing the Personal Information Forms in Element 4. Allow time for students to review the club selections and fill in both parts of the form. Be sure they understand that they are to rank their preferences.

D. EL HORARIO

Help students review the vocabulary of the school subjects and extracurricular clubs. You may wish to make flash cards of your own (such as those suggested for students in Activities A and B). Use the cards for vocabulary drill, but try to find ways in which the vocabulary may be contextualized. For example, do a TPR activity with each student using the small flash cards. Ask students to arrange cards in a certain order on their desk. You say, **Pon la ciencia a la izquierda de la natación.** Students arrange the cards by placing the card representing science to the left of the card representing the swimming club. You may also wish to ask them to do a variety of actions with the cards, such as placing them in different locations around the room or giving them to another student. Refer to the TPR suggestions with table-setting items in Element 8. When students are comfortable with the vocabulary, allow time for them to complete the schedule card.

E. PAPEL, LÁPIZ Y LIBRO

Go through the directions with the class. Allow time for pair practice. Review the use of **un** and **una** *(a, an)*. Remind students of the numeral **uno** *(one)*. Tell them to complete the exercise by finding the object in the picture and putting the letter of the object in the blank next to the Spanish word.

Answer Key:

1. un cuaderno *(a notebook)*   E
2. un lápiz *(a pencil)*   D
3. un bolígrafo *(a pen)*   F
4. un libro *(a book)*   I
5. una hoja de papel *(a piece of paper)*   J
6. un sacapuntas *(a pencil sharpener)*   C
7. una regla *(a ruler)*   L
8. una mochila *(a backpack)*   H
9. una calculadora *(a calculator)*   B
10. una goma *(an eraser)*   A
11. un marcador *(a marker)*   K
12. un cartelón *(a piece of poster board)*   G

EXPANSION

If it is age and developmentally appropriate, you may wish to expand this activity in the following ways:

- Point out the comparison of the use of **un** and **una** with **el** and **la**. Give students a very simple explanation of the difference between *a* or *an* as opposed to *the*. Remind them that more than one of **el** is **los**, more than one of **la** is **las** (all four forms mean *the*), and more than one of **un** and **una** are **unos** and **unas** *(some)*.

- Review the formation of plurals of the names of objects (nouns). This information was presented in Element 2. You may wish to give students the following formula. Words ending in a vowel *(a, e, i, o, u)* add -*s*. Words ending in a consonant add -*es*. Words ending in *z* such as lápiz, change the *z*, to *c* and add -*es* (lápices).

EXPANSION

Memory Game. (BLM 10.1) This game provides additional practice with the vocabulary for classroom objects presented in this Element. The game is played with 24 playing cards cut from the Blackline Master. Twelve of the cards show a picture of a classroom object. The other twelve contain the corresponding Spanish vocabulary. All cards are placed face down. The object of the game is for the players to match the picture card with the corresponding vocabulary card. As each player turns two cards face up, the cards must match or they are turned face down again. Subsequent players try to remember the location of the cards.

Directions for playing the game:

Have scissors available and duplicate enough copies of **BLM 10.1** for each group to have one copy.

- Divide students into groups of two to four.

- Give one copy of the Blackline Master to each group.

- Have the groups cut the Blackline Master into 24 individual cards (12 picture cards and 12 vocabulary cards).

- Students in each group place all cards face down on the table or desktop. The cards should be mixed well. Once placed, the cards remain in the same position.

- Player A selects two cards and turns them over for the other players to see. If the two cards match (a picture and its corresponding word), Player A keeps the pair and gets one point. If the cards do not match, they are once again turned face down. Then the other players take their turns. This continues until all cards have been matched.

- Points are tallied, and winners are declared.

VARIATION

Make up additional cards to recycle vocabulary from other activities in this and other Elements (school subjects, extracurricular activities, table-setting items, household furniture and other items, etc.).

F. PRÁCTICA

Go over the directions with students. Allow sufficient time for them to complete the exercise. Verify the answers with the class.

Answer Key:

1. MATEMÁTICAS   f
2. LIBRO   e
3. CIENCIA   g
4. GEOGRAFÍA   h

5. LÁPIZ a

6. GOMA d

7. ESPAÑOL c

8. GIMNASIA b

EXPANSION

Have students complete **BLM 10.2.**

EXPANSION

Make up additional scrambled words. Put them on the board or an overhead transparency. As students come into class, they work on the activity while you are completing attendance and other housekeeping chores.

EXPANSION

Allow students to make up additional word scrambles. Duplicate copies and have students complete them in class or as an out-of-class activity.

EXPANSION

Team competition. Each team makes up a set of scrambled words. A student volunteer puts the scrambled word on a clear acetate, using the overhead projector while the projector light is off. The light is turned on, and the team to unscramble the word first gets ten points. The first team to reach 100 wins.

G. LAS MATERIAS Y LOS CLUBES: ¿CUÁL TE GUSTA MÁS?

Present the three sentences. If you prepared flash cards for Activities A and B, use them to elicit answers to the questions. You may wish to begin by holding up a picture representing a school subject or club and say, for example, **Me gusta más el español,** while pointing to yourself. Repeat this several times and then ask the class to repeat after you. Hold up different cards and ask the question, ¿**Cuál materia (club) te gusta más?** Have all of the students answer as a group. When they seem comfortable with the vocabulary, ask for individual volunteers to respond. Do not use the cards at this point. Authentic questions require an information or opinion gap. When you ask the question, you do not know which subject or club the student prefers. Finally, allow time for pair practice or a chain drill in which Student A asks the question and Student B responds.

Go over the directions for taking the poll with the class. Give students a day or more to gather the information. Allow class time for reporting. If students have done charts and graphs, put these on a bulletin board or on a sheet of tagboard or poster board.

EXTENSION

Mathematics. Have students compile the results of the poll. Then have them convert the results into percentages.

EXTENSION

BLM 10.3. Duplicate enough copies of the tally sheet for each student to have a copy. Tell students to take a poll by interviewing ten different classmates. Explain that they should use the symbols to indicate each classmate's ranking of the classes.

H. ¿CÓMO ES TU ESCUELA? (BLM 10.4)

Present the title question and practice it with the class. You may wish to introduce or review some simple words or phrases to answer the question. Example: **Es grande. Es pequeña. Hay muchos estudiantes.**

Review the seven steps with the class. Duplicate and distribute one copy of the checklist (**BLM 10.4**) per student. The types of projects will depend on the age, ability, and developmental level of students. This project offers an opportunity for each student to excel. Encourage individuality and creativity. The activity is designed as an individual project; however, if you have students who are unable to handle this type of assignment, you may wish to allow them to work in pairs or small groups. Be sure to clarify the method of evaluation to be used for pair or group projects (group grade vs. individual grades and criteria for grading).

Step 1: Brainstorm, select, outline, and define the project (four phases).

- Go over the idea map. Remind students that in brainstorming, any and all ideas are acceptable. Tell them to write all of their ideas on a sheet of paper.

- The students review their ideas and select the ones they want to put in the cells of the map. They do not need to be restricted to the four cells. Some students may be capable of adding more cells. For others, it may be appropriate for them to work with only two topics.

- The index card is designed to lead students to organize their ideas in a logical sequence for presentation. Have them write the topics in the order in which they plan to present them.

- The type of presentation should be limited only by the imagination of students. They should be encouraged to select a presentation format of interest to them. You may wish to suggest projects incorporating any of the following:

  written or oral reports

  skits

  musical presentations (such as the school song)

  comic-strip art

  posters

  display of photographs

  video

Consider any format appropriate to the age and developmental level of students, as well as the resources available to them.

Step 2: Shopping List

Introduce and model the phrase **ir de compras.** Have English-Spanish dictionaries available. Help students compile a list of the materials they will need to complete their projects.

Step 3: Art

All students should be encouraged to incorporate some form of drawing, photograph, artwork, or other visuals into their projects. This is a perfect opportunity for those students who are artistically talented to excel.

Step 4: Labeling

Labeling allows students to use vocabulary. It does not require complex syntax involving grammatical structures. Accept single words and short phrases as long as they are used appropriately.

Step 5: Practice

Encourage students to work in pairs or small groups to practice presenting their projects. Transescent learners may be extremely apprehensive about talking in front of a large group. The opportunity to practice can help them build self-confidence. It will be helpful for you to review each project prior to the final presentation.

Step 6: Project Presentation

Schedule several projects to be presented each day over a period of a week. Allow ample time for the presentations. If you have students who are extremely apprehensive about speaking in front of the entire class, you may wish to allow them to present their projects to a small group. Encourage them, but do not insist that they give their presentations to the entire class.

Step 7: Grading

Review the grading scale with the class. Help students translate the 1–10 scale into the grading system used in your school or class. Decide what factors you will consider in grading and discuss them with students. Consider effort, organization, the way in which they followed the seven-step process, and their use of the Spanish language. Allow students to evaluate their own projects and decide what grade they think they should receive. Review their self-evaluation and decide on an appropriate grade.

I. MI DIARIO

Tell students to review the entire Element before beginning this activity. You may wish to go over the vocabulary from the various activities. Encourage students to be creative and to include as much Spanish as possible. Refer to the **Mi diario** sections in previous Elements for additional suggestions and ideas about using this activity.

11 SIGHTSEEING

Picture card #11 "Bus trip" may be used with this element.

Contents

1. **Communicative Functions:**

   Imparting and seeking factual information (reporting, asking) expressing likes, dislikes, and preferences

2. **Content and Language Skills:**

   Ground transportation, vocabulary for taking a subway (metro), expressions of weather, Fahrenheit and Celsius temperatures

3. **Culture:**

   Major points of interest in some Spanish-speaking countries, riding the subway in Mexico City or Madrid

4. **Teaching and Learning Strategies:**

   Predicting, researching, using TPR, cooperative learning, reporting, surveying, comparing, following directions, note taking

Additional Activity Suggestions (Extension and Interdisciplinary)

1. **Extension**

   - Have students contact local travel agencies or embassies of Spanish-speaking countries for tourist brochures. Review and discuss the kinds of information in them.

   - Invite a local meteorologist to discuss weather, weather forecasting, and a global perspective of weather.

   - Have students obtain subway maps of some major cities in the United States (Washington, D.C., New York City) and have students compare them with those presented in this Element.

2. **Science**

   - Arrange for a trip to a weather station or local television station.

   - Work with the science teacher in your building to develop projects related to weather.

3. **Speech and Drama**

   - Have students work in small groups to develop skits incorporating themes of sightseeing, weather, and recreational activities.

4. **Social Studies**

   - Have students do research on the famous places for which metro stops are named in Mexico City or Madrid (other than those presented for research possibility in the lesson).

5. **Advisor/Advisee or Homeroom**

   • Discuss the uses of public transportation. What are some of the issues surrounding its use, such as personal safety, cost, and availability?

   • Obtain copies of brochures and tourist literature about your town or city from the local chamber of commerce. Discuss the kinds of information included in them. Have students talk about whether or not they feel this is an accurate representation of their town.

PERSPECTIVA

The **Perspectiva** is an advance organizer intended to stimulate discussion about the topics to be covered in this Element. Draw the attention of students to the two sections of the page, as well as the border design. (You may wish to use **BLM 11.0** for this activity.) The discussion should surround topics of tourist brochures, types of transportation, and weather.

A. PUNTOS DE INTERÉS

Activities A and B are closely connected. Review the list of places in Activity A with students. Draw their attention to the cognates to help them guess what the sites might be. When they have finished their predictions, go through the list and give them the basic identification of each one. Go on to Activity B (locations of these sites) before directing students to any reference sources.

Answer Key:

1.	El Museo del Prado	museum	Spain
2.	El Palacio de las Bellas Artes	theater	Mexico
3.	El Morro	fortress	Puerto Rico
4.	El Alcázar	castle	Spain
5.	El Parque de Chapultepec	park	Mexico
6.	Machu Picchu	Incan ruins site	Peru
7.	El Museo Nacional de Antropología	museum	Mexico
8.	El Parque del Retiro	park	Spain
9.	La Alhambra	ancient Moorish palace	Spain
10.	La Quebrada	site of cliff divers	Mexico
11.	Chichén Itzá	ancient Mayan ruins	Mexico
12.	Lago Titicaca	lake	Bolivia, Peru
13.	Los Pirineos	mountains	Spain
14.	El Volcán Poás	volcano	Costa Rica
15.	El Zócalo	central city square	Mexico

B. ¿DÓNDE ESTÁN LOS PUNTOS DE INTERÉS?

Use gestures and TPR to introduce the question: **¿Dónde están?** *(Where are they?)* You may wish to conduct a brief practice using classroom items. Give some items to several student volunteers (pencils, books, notebooks, etc.). Prepare them beforehand to reply when you ask for the items. Example: You ask, **¿Dónde están los libros?** The student to whom you have given the books holds them up or walks to the front of the room and gives them to you, saying, **Aquí están**, or **Aquí están los libros.**

Proceed with the activity. Arrange for the class to use the library or media center. Encourage students to select different sites. This will ensure that the class receives information about all of the locations. Set aside classtime over a period of several days for reports and other forms of presentation. It is difficult for transescent learners to remain focused on any one activity for a prolonged time period. Using several days for the exercise breaks the monotony and enhances the possibility of their learning from the material as it is presented by their classmates.

Explain to students that they should use the card in their book to take notes on the information as it is given by others. Discuss the concept of note taking. You may wish to do an example on the board or an overhead transparency. Be sure students understand that they do not need to remember all of the facts presented. They should, however, write down pertinent information about the sites and facts that are of particular interest to them.

Circulate among students as the reports are being given. Check to see that they understand the directions and are taking notes appropriately.

EXPANSION

Small-group activity. Once all reports and presentations have been given, allow time for students to work in groups of three to five. Have them compare the notes and information they put on their cards. Students can then determine if anyone is missing facts or has discrepancies in the information noted by other members of the group. Have them make a list of questions or consult the individual who gave the report. Finally, conduct a class discussion on the places, their locations, history, and significance to the country. Ask students to talk about what they learned. Have them indicate one or two of the places they might especially like to visit and give the reasons for their choice. If students have done posters or other forms of visual reports, provide a bulletin board or other appropriate space as a display area.

EXPANSION

Vamos a visitar los puntos de interés. (BLM 11.1) Divide the class into teams of two students. Duplicate sufficient copies of the Blackline Master. Prepare the dominoes and place them in envelopes containing one set of dominoes for each team. Then give students the following directions:

How much can you remember about where **los puntos de interés** are located? Choose a partner for this domino game. Each domino is divided in half. One half has the name of a point of interest. On the other half is the name of a country where one of the sites is located. The object of the game is to match all of your dominoes. Here are the rules:

1. Turn all of the dominoes face down on the table.

2. Each player chooses seven dominoes.

3. Player A lays down one of his or her dominoes, face up.

4. Player B must match one half of that domino with one of his or her dominoes. If player B cannot make a match, he or she must pick one domino from the remaining dominoes on the table.

5. Player A continues in the same way.

6. The game ends when:

  • Someone matches all of his or her dominoes, or

  • No one can play because there are no matches for the remaining face-up dominoes.

In the second case, the player with the fewest dominoes in his or her hand is declared the winner. ¡Buena suerte!

C. MODOS DE TRANSPORTACIÓN

Introduce the vocabulary, including the activity title and **una excursión**.

1. **la motocicleta**   motorbike/motorcycle

2. **el autobús**   bus

3. **el metro**   subway/metro

4. **el auto**   automobile

5. **el tren**   train

When students are comfortable with the vocabulary, review the survey form with them. The survey may be completed within the class, or you may wish to have students get information from others in the school. If they get information from students who are not taking Spanish, encourage them to teach the Spanish vocabulary to those whom they survey.

EXPANSION

Flash cards. Using 3 X 5 index cards, have students cut out or draw pictures depicting various kinds of transportation. Have them write the corresponding Spanish term on the reverse side of the card. Allow time for pair work to practice the vocabulary. Student A shows the picture side of the card to Student B. Student B gives the Spanish vocabulary for the method of transportation. Then students switch roles. The cards can be placed in the students' word box/bank started in earlier Elements. Students may use a dictionary or consult earlier Elements for additional methods of transportation (**el avión**/airplane, **el patín**/skateboard, **la motoneta**/moped, etc.).

EXPANSION

Mathematics. Have students make a chart or graph showing the results of the survey. The charts or graphs should show the preferred mode of transportation and some of the reasons given for the choices.

D. ¿EL METRO? ¿QUÉ ES?

Read the introductory part of this activity with students. Familiarize them with the Spanish vocabulary. Then allow time for them to read silently through the eight sentences. Next, read the sentences aloud in Spanish. Pause long enough for students to write in their predictions of the English meanings. Finally, read the sentences a second time to verify the responses. Ask for student volunteers to give responses or have all of the students respond in unison.

Answer Key:

1. the entrance (entry)

2. the subway or metro, a ticket

3. your ticket, a ticket window

4. direction

5. a transfer

6. metro stations

7. stop or station, the exit

8. an exit, ticket

EXPANSION

Vocabulary. You may wish to give the following additional vocabulary used with subway travel:

cambiar	to change
bajar	to get off
una línea	(subway) line or route
un boleto	ticket
una parada	subway stop or station
un billete sencillo	single ticket
un billete de diez viajes	book of ten tickets
una tarjeta de abono transportes	one-month commuter pass
un metrotour de tres días	three-day tourist ticket (also available for five days)

EXPANSION

Role play. Set up a ticket window. One student plays the role of the traveler (**pasajero/a**), and the other, the role of the employee (**empleado/a**):

La pasajera: Por favor, señor, un billete de diez viajes.

El empleado: Cuatrocientas cincuenta pesetas, señorita.

La pasajera: Gracias, señor.

The dialogue can be varied and expanded depending on the age and developmental level of your students. Students can also make mock metro tickets from paper or cardstock.

E. UNA EXCURSIÓN EN EL METRO

Review the names of the metro stops. The names are all names of famous sites or Spanish-speaking individuals presented earlier in this or other Elements. Review the metro map with students. Then have them answer the questions.

Answer Key:

Mexico City

1. no

2. **Pantitlán**

3. 12

Madrid

1. sí

2. **Cuatro Caminos**

3. 8

EXPANSION

Make up a variety of situations using both maps, and have students answer the questions based on the new situation. You may also wish to have students make up situations. They may give these to you to present to the class, or they may wish to present the situations themselves.

EXPANSION

Have students work in pairs or small groups. Tell them to consult a guidebook for Mexico City (such as *Fodor's, Frommer's,* etc.) and find a number of tourist attractions in the city. Have them determine which metro stop is closest to each attraction.

F. ¿QUÉ TIEMPO HACE?

Present the question **¿Qué tiempo hace?** Ask students to look at the pictures as you say the expressions in Spanish. Next, say the expressions again and have students repeat them after you. Then allow a brief period of time for pair practice. Finally, say the expressions again. As you say each one, have students point to the picture that corresponds to the type of weather you are describing in Spanish. Circulate among students as you do this to verify their responses and to ascertain if there are any problems in comprehension. Have each student complete the sentence in his or her book. Students should select a favorite kind of weather and give a statement supporting their choice.

EXPANSION

Vocabulary: **Me gusta el tiempo cuando...** *(I like the weather when . . .)*

EXPANSION

Flash cards. Using 3 × 5 index cards, have students cut out or draw pictures depicting each kind of weather. Have them write the corresponding Spanish expression on the reverse side of the card. Allow time for pair work to practice the vocabulary. Student A shows the picture side of the card to Student B. Student B gives the Spanish expression for the weather. Then students switch roles. The cards can be placed in each student's word box/bank started in earlier Elements.

EXPANSION

Art. Clothing Match. (BLM 2.1) Supplies needed: Copies of **BLM 2.1**, old magazines and catalogues, tape, glue, scissors, markers, crayons, construction paper, poster board, tagboard, and shirt cardboard.

This activity will recycle the vocabulary for articles of clothing introduced in Element 2. The purpose is to have students review the articles of clothing in Spanish and match the appropriate clothing to the weather. Have students draw or cut out and label the various articles of clothing. They can make individual posters or a collage. Each one should feature a type of weather, pictured and written in Spanish. The appropriate articles of clothing or people dressed in that clothing are placed on the poster or in the picture. Articles of clothing should be labeled in Spanish.

EXTENSION

Video report. This activity will depend on the age and developmental level of students as well as available resources. You may wish to have them work with the school media specialist and make a video report. Have students work in pairs or groups and make a videotape of various kinds of weather. As they show the tape to the class, they describe the weather in Spanish. If the video also shows people, then have them describe what the people are wearing in relation to the weather. They may not be able to use complete sentences or complex structures; however, they can identify the articles of clothing and the weather.

G. UNA COMPARACIÓN DE TEMPERATURAS

Read the introductory paragraph with students. Have them look at the thermometer and make some comparison of Celsius to Fahrenheit temperatures. Then have them go through the Celsius temperatures given and convert them into Fahrenheit. You may wish to give them the following formula to verify their responses:

To convert Celsius to Fahrenheit:

1. Multiply by 9.

2. Divide by 5.

3. Add 32.

Answer Key:

1. 50° F

2. 75.2° F

3. 86° F

4. 89.6° F

5. 68° F

6. 37.4° F

EXPANSION

Mathematics. Temperature Conversions. In addition to the conversion formula above, give students the following formula for converting Fahrenheit to Celsius:

1. Subtract 32 from the Fahrenheit temperature.

2. Multiply by 5.

3. Divide by 9.

Here are some suggested temperatures. Have students work in pairs. Using the above formulas, have them convert the temperatures into either Celsius or Farenheit.

1. el 1 de enero   12° C = <u>53.6</u>° F

2. el 5 de febrero   17° C = <u>62.6</u>° F

3. el 21 de marzo   22° C = <u>71.6</u>° F

4. el 5 de mayo   25° C = <u>77</u>° F

5 June 17th   79° F = <u>26.1</u>° C

6. August 24th   88° F = <u>31.1</u>° C

7. September 16th   67° F = <u>19.4</u>° C

8. November 20th   54° F = <u>12.2</u>° C

EXPANSION

Have students make up additional temperatures for conversion.

EXPANSION

Have students look up the average monthly temperatures for their own city and their homestay city. Then ask them to chart a comparison indicating whether the temperatures are higher, lower, or about the same.

H. LAS ACTIVIDADES Y LA TEMPERATURA

This activity recycles some vocabulary presented in Element 4. Ask students to look at the pictures of the activities scattered on the page. Next, read the list in Spanish, pausing after each activity. Then have students repeat the phrases after you. Students should work on their own or with a partner to predict the English meanings of the phrases. After they have completed their predictions, verify the meanings with them. You may do this by asking for individual volunteers to respond or the class to respond as a group.

Next, have students write the letter of each picture next to the Spanish term it illustrates.

Answer Key:

1. watching a video   f

2. swimming   h

3. walking   b

4. playing baseball   a

5. riding a horse   c

6. going shopping   d

7. riding a bicycle to the park   i

8. canoeing   e

9. going to the movies   g

Review the phrase **me gusta**, and have students practice saying (or writing) their favorite activities. This can be done as a chain exercise. You start by asking one student **¿Qué te gusta?** and model a response beginning, **Me gusta...**, or show a picture or a photo of one of the activities and say **Me gusta...** and supply the phrase that corresponds to the picture. Then turn to a student and ask, ¿Y tú? That student replies, and then asks a classmate. Finally, have students complete the sentences at the end of the activity. Answers will vary. You may wish to suggest that students review activities presented in Element 4.

I. ¡VAMOS A PLANEAR LAS ACTIVIDADES!

Again, you may wish to review activities from Element 4 or suggest that students do so. You may also wish to have Spanish-English dictionaries available for this activity. Review the directions for the activity with the class. Have students review the days of the week, weather expressions, temperature conversions, and possible activities. Allow time for them to complete the activity as directed. Answers will vary; however, check for logical responses. For example, it would not be logical to select **nadar** *(going swimming)* on **lunes** when the temperature is 7° C (45° F), unless they specify going to an indoor pool.

J. MI DIARIO

If you have been meeting with your students for several weeks, then they are familiar with this culminating activity. They should be comfortable using vocabulary from the various Elements. Encourage them to use as much Spanish as they can. Allow for their using interlanguage and experimentation with the vocabulary they have learned. Emphasize the appropriate use of lexicon rather than the syntax and grammar. Refer to this section in previous Elements for additional suggestions.

12 A BIRTHDAY PARTY

Picture cards 12 "Birthday party" and 5b "Boy wrapping present" may be used with this element.

Contents

1. **Communicative Functions:**

   Imparting and seeking factual information (identifying and asking), socializing, getting things done, expressing want or desire, expressing and finding out emotional attitudes (liking, disliking), inquiring about preference

2. **Content and Language Skills:**

   Interrogatives (**por qué, quién, cuándo, dónde, cuánto**), vocabulary associated with birthday celebration, numbers 100–1,000,000; shopping, ordering, and foods in a fast-food restaurant

3. **Culture:**

   Appropriate expressions and gifts for birthdays, **piñatas**

4. **Teaching and Learning Strategies:**

   Playing games, role play, using TPR, cooperative learning (jigsaw), webbing thematically, buying and selling items, counting, ordering food, group planning, idea mapping

Additional Activity Suggestions (Extension and Interdisciplinary)

1. **Extension**

   - Discuss the concept of individual shops and stores as opposed to large department stores or supermarkets.

   - Make a list of English expressions commonly used in birthday cards and at birthday celebrations and compare them to Spanish.

2. **Mathematics**

   - Set up a shop or store. Have students take turns being the shopkeeper or the customer. Customers use play money or Monopoly money and decide how much they can spend on a given number of items. The shopkeeper must make change and provide receipts.

   - Have students call the local bank for the current rate of exchange between **pesos (NP/N$)** and dollars. Then practice converting prices from dollars to **pesos (NP/N$)**.

3. **Home Economics**

   - Discuss food groups and the concept of good nutrition.

   - Categorize fast-food items and obtain information about their nutritional content.

   - Bake and decorate a birthday cake.

4. **Art**

   - Have students make a piñata.

5. **Advisor/Advisee or Homeroom**

   - Discuss the role of fast food in U.S. society. How does it affect nutrition?

   - Have students talk about what has happened to the concept of mealtime as an opportunity for family members to discuss and share ideas and concerns.

   - Discuss gift giving. When do people give gifts? What kinds of gifts are appropriate? Does this differ according to cultural or ethnic background?

   - Discuss the significant age markers or "rites of passage" in U.S. society (voting age, military draft eligibility, driver's license, PG-13 movies, etc.).

PERSPECTIVA

The **Perspectiva** is intended to be an advance organizer to stimulate discussion about the topic to be covered in this Element. Ask students to look at the two sections. (You may wish to use **BLM 12.0** for this activity.) Have students guess the meaning of **Feliz cumpleaños**. Draw their attention to the word **años** that they learned earlier. Have them look at the storefronts and guess the meaning of each name: **Florería**/*florist*, **Joyería**/*jewelry store*, **Librería**/*bookstore* (not *library*), **Tienda de música**/*music store*, and **Pastelería**/*bakery* or *cake shop*. (Point out that a **pastelería** is different from a **panadería**, where only bread is sold.) Many Spanish-speaking towns and cities still have individual shops and stores. There are large all-purpose stores or supermarkets in many of the larger cities; however, the smaller neighborhoods and small towns still have their own specialty shops.

A. LA INVITACIÓN

Students should easily recognize the title of this activity as a cognate. Have them look at the four interrogatives presented on the invitation. Draw their attention to the words following each and have them guess the meaning of the question word or words. Begin with **¿quién?**/*who?*, **¿cuándo?**/*when?*, or **¿dónde?**/*where?*, as the meaning may be more apparent. Then move **¿por qué?**/*why?* Once you have verified the meanings, pronounce each interrogative in Spanish and have students repeat them after you.

Una fiesta, names, days, dates, and addresses are recycled from earlier Elements. **Cumpleaños** *(birthday)* is new vocabulary. If the question is raised, and if it is age and developmentally appropriate, give a brief explanation of the use of birthday as a collective noun. Do not overemphasize the grammatical point. The same caveat applies to the explanation of the accent marks on the interrogatives. Tell students that they may see and use these same words without the accent marks. Without them, the words lose their interrogative meaning. Make a quick word game of **¿Por qué?** *(why?)* and **porque** *(because)*. This is also a good time to point out the use of voice inflection to differentiate between a statement (the voice stays the same or drops) and a question (upward inflection).

Draw students' attention to **¡Celebremos!** and the meaning *Let's celebrate!* From this, as well as the frequent use of **¡Vámonos!** throughout these materials, students may deduce that **-amos** and **-nos** are grammatical markers for *we* and *us*.

Tell students that they will have an opportunity to create an invitation later in this Element. They will be asked to do this as part of the planning for a birthday party in Activity I.

EXPANSION

Interdisciplinary — Art. Have a variety of art supplies available for this activity. Have each student design and create an invitation using his or her own personal birthday information. Provide bulletin board space or another display area for the finished invitations.

B. UNA TARJETA (BLM 12.1)

Go through the list of expressions with students. Model the phrases and have students repeat them after you. Allow some time for pair, small-group, as well as whole-group repetition and practice.

Para mi amigo Enrique	For my friend Henry
¡Feliz cumpleaños!	Happy birthday!
¡Que pases un cumpleaños feliz!	Have a happy birthday!
¡Buena suerte!	Good luck!
¡Que pases un día estupendo!	Have a great day!
¡Diviértete!	Have fun!
¡Gozas!	Enjoy!
Un abrazo	A hug (I give you a hug)
Con cariño	With affection (affectionately)
Tu amigo/a	Your friend (masculine/feminine)

Once students are comfortable with the Spanish pronunciation, go through the expressions and have students give the meanings in English. Then proceed to the following matching card activity to reinforce the meanings and provide further practice. Duplicate enough copies of **BLM 12.1** for each student to have a set of the cards. The cards will be more durable if printed on cardstock. You may wish to cut them into halves prior to distribution or allow students to cut their own set. Have students shuffle the card pieces after they are cut and then tell them to try to match the Spanish and English halves. Remind them to say the Spanish phrase quietly to themselves whenever they match a set. Allow ample time for individual and pair practice.

Finally, provide a variety of art supplies. Have each student design and create a birthday card. Circulate among students to ensure that they have an idea of what they wish to do, and help them select a phrase or phrases in Spanish to use on the card. The card making may take more than one class period. Allow ample time for completion of the activity. Encourage students to repeat, sing, or otherwise practice the Spanish expressions during the time they are creating their cards. Provide bulletin board space or another display area for the finished cards. This is also an excellent project to send home with students or to display for parent visitation.

C. IDEAS PARA UN REGALO

This activity recycles vocabulary from earlier Elements. First, ask students to read the list of items. Give them time to work with a partner or in small group to verify the meanings in English. Then go through the list with the entire class. Say the Spanish for each item and have students call out the English meaning. Next, say the Spanish again, having students repeat after you. Allow time for students to complete the matching activity. Review the list again and have a student volunteer or the entire class verify the matches.

Answer Key:

1.	un disco	f
2.	un reloj	k
3.	una bicicleta	a
4.	una guitarra	e
5.	un piano	i
6.	una camiseta	c
7.	un radio	b
8.	un casette	d
9.	un juego de video	h
10.	una motocicleta	l
11.	un disco compacto	j
12.	una sudadera	g

EXPANSION

If students have not already done so in earlier Elements, have them make small flash cards for the suggested gift items. Have magazines, catalogues, and drawing supplies available. Students can make flash cards of the various gift items by pasting pictures on 3 × 5 index cards. They should write the Spanish name of the item on the back of the card. Larger flash cards can be made using shirt cardboard. These flash cards can be used for individual or pair practice. The smaller cards can be placed in the word box/bank, as suggested in Element 1.

Next, allow time for students to write some of their ideas for a gift in the space resembling a scrap of paper. Circulate around the room as they are doing this part of the activity to be sure that they are completing the task.

Finally, work with the entire class or allow students to work in pairs or small groups to complete the idea map. You may wish to do the activity on a blank overhead transparency or give each small group or pair of students a blank transparency. Have them complete the task on the transparency and then project their ideas for the entire class.

EXTENSION

Art. Bring in a variety of boxes, wrapping paper, tape, scissors and ribbon. Have students wrap the "presents." Extension vocabulary:

¡Pon!	Put!
¡Envuelve!	Wrap!
la caja	box
el papel decorado	wrapping paper
el papel de envolver	wrapping paper
la cinta	tape
el cordón	ribbon

VARIATION

TPR. Use a small box, ribbon, and a piece of paper. Give students the directions to place the items in various locations on their desktop. This will give you an opportunity to recycle the location vocabulary from Element 8.

VARIATION

Have students draw the wrapped presents. Recycle the vocabulary for colors from Element 2.

D. NÚMEROS PARA LAS COMPRAS

Remind students that they learned the numbers from 1 to 100 in Elements 2 and 5. (If they have not studied these Elements, you will need to present those numbers before proceeding with this activity.) Allow time for review and practice of these numbers using any of the techniques suggested for their initial presentation. You may wish to do this first with the entire class and then allow time for pair practice.

Next, ask students to look at the row of numbers in their book. Dictate the numbers in random order. Repeat each number twice. Allow time for students to cross out the number. Then give the correct number in English or ask for a student volunteer or total class response.

12	doce
24	veinticuatro
37	treinta y siete
48	cuarenta y ocho
59	cincuenta y nueve
60	sesenta
65	sesenta y cinco
70	setenta
79	setenta y nueve
81	ochenta y uno
93	noventa y tres
100	cien

Finally, review numbers 100 to 1,000 (first introduced in Element 5), and then introduce the remaining numbers: ten thousand, one hundred thousand, and one million. Point out to students that in many countries a space or period is used for place value instead of a comma. Again, use a variety of techniques and methods for drill and practice. It is most important to remember that the learner needs to be able to recognize the numbers when he or she hears them. The ability to produce the Spanish words for the numerals follows the recognition. It is also worth noting that individuals will almost always resort to doing mathematical calculations and counting in their first or native language.

E. ¿CUÁNTO ES?

Introduce the phrase and model it in Spanish. Proceed with the sentence **¿Cuánto cuesta un disco compacto?** Allow time for students to fill in the blanks in their text.

F. EL PRECIO (BLM 12.2)

Introduce the vocabulary and the concept of different forms of money.

Duplicate one copy of the Blackline Master for each student. Cut the price tags out and put one set in an envelope for each student. (You may wish to have students cut out the tags and place them in an envelope.) Have students arrange the price tags on their desks in order from the smallest to the largest amount.

Proceed with the dictation. Depending on the age and developmental level of students, you may wish to do this task in two phases. First, dictate the name of the item in Spanish and allow time for students to write the Spanish term on the line below the drawing of the item. Second, repeat the name of the item and using the word **cuesta**, give its price. Students then place the price tag next to the item. The following are some suggested sentences. You may wish to vary the prices or dictate the items in a more random order. Tell students that the prices will not necessarily be realistic in terms of actual dollar equivalents.

1. Un disco compacto cuesta veinticinco (25) pesos.

2. Un reloj cuesta ciento cincuenta (150) pesos.

3. Una bicicleta cuesta quinientos (500) pesos.

4. Una guitarra cuesta cuatrocientos (400) pesos.

5. Un piano cuesta tres mil (3.000) pesos.

6. Una camiseta cuesta quince (15) pesos.

7. Un radio cuesta trescientos (300) pesos.

8. Un casette cuesta cuarenta y cinco (45) pesos.

9. Un juego de video cuesta doscientos (200) pesos.

10. Una motocicleta cuesta seis mil (6.000) pesos.

11. Una sudadera cuesta cincuenta y tres (53) pesos.

12. Un disco cuesta treinta (30) pesos.

EXTENSION

Have students research the unit of currency in one or more Spanish-speaking countries. You may wish to have them select the same country they chose in Element 1 as their homestay country.

EXTENSION

Interdisciplinary/Mathematics. Have students research the unit of currency in one or more Spanish-speaking countries. Have them call the local bank and obtain the current rate(s) of exchange. Using the items in this activity, have them make up a chart listing first the price in dollars, followed by the equivalent in pesos and one or more additional units of currency.

G. EL JUEGO DE COMPRAS

BLM 12.3 and BLM 12.4. BLM 12.3 contains the picture cards to be duplicated and cut apart. Make sufficient quantities for each student to select five cards. BLM 12.4 contains the money. You may also wish to use other "play money" such as Monopoly money. Make sufficient copies of BLM 12.4 for each student to have an envelope with 2.500 NP/N$ divided as follows:

one	1.000
one	500
five	100
six	50
five	20
eight	10
four	5

The objective of the game is for students to purchase the objects on their list and have money remaining. Remind students to use as much Spanish as they can. **NOTA:** *Regatear* means *to barter* in Spanish. Bartering is an interesting facet of life in the Spanish-speaking world. Remind students that major establishments have fixed prices, as do stores in the United States. Bartering takes place in the marketplaces and small shops.

Review all of the directions with students. Practice the Spanish phrases **me gustaría** *(I would like)*, **por favor** *(please)*, **¿Cuánto es?** *(How much is it?)* and **¿Cuánto cuesta?** *(How much does it cost?)*

Allow each student to select five picture cards. On the back of the card they are to write 1) the Spanish terms for the items presented in Activity C on page 134 of their text and 2) their "asking price" for each item. Circulate among students as they are completing this phase of the preparation to answer questions and to help them determine the prices they wish to ask. You may wish to have them write both the numeral and the Spanish words for the prices.

Finally, play the game. Allow sufficient time for students to circulate, buy, and sell the items. At the end of the allotted time (which you determine based on the age, developmental and interest level of students), ask for volunteers to tell the class the Spanish names of the items they purchased and how much money they have left.

EXTENSION

Review. Set up a store in a corner of the classroom. Stock it with merchandise and articles representing any of the vocabulary students have learned in previous Elements. The merchandise may be actual items or realia and replicas. Students take turns being the shopkeeper and the customer. Some suggestions for merchandise are school supplies, table-setting items, and household furnishings. Have students decide which unit of currency (other than dollars) will be used in the store. Use Monopoly money or have students make play money.

H. FAST FOOD

Introduce the vocabulary **¡Tengo hambre!** and **una merienda.** Tell students that the term *fast food* is used in Spanish-speaking countries as well. If possible, bring to class the actual item or a plastic or paper facsimile. Use these or another form of realia to present the vocabulary. You may also wish to make flash cards with pictures of the items to use in your presentation. Cardboard from new shirts or a drycleaning establishment are sturdy, a nice size to handle, and easily seen by students. In this case, it would be more authentic to use a paper plate as a flash card backing.

Vocabulary:

hamburguesa/*hamburger*

hamburguesa con queso/*cheeseburger*

pollo/*chicken*

filete de pescado/*fish sandwich*

papas fritas (chico, mediano, grande)/*french fries (small, medium, large)*

café/*coffee*

leche/*milk*

jugo de naranja/*orange juice*

coca/*Coke*

coca de dieta/*diet coke*

naranja/*orange soda*

Proceed to the dialogue between the employee (**empleado/a**) and the customer (**cliente**).

¿Qué quieres?	*What would you like?*
Me gustaría _____, por favor.	*I would like _____, please.*
Sí, gracias.	*Yes, thank you.*
No, _____, por favor.	*No, _____, please.*

Practice the vocabulary with students, using the dialogue phrases. When students seem reasonably comfortable with the words, allow time for pair practice.

EXPANSION

Have magazines, catalogues, and drawing supplies available. Students can make flash cards of the various menu items by pasting pictures on 3 × 5 index cards. They should write the Spanish vocabulary on the reverse side of the card. Larger flash cards can be made using shirt cardboard. These flash cards can be used for individual or pair practice. The smaller cards can be placed in the word box/bank, as suggested in Element 1.

I.   LA FIESTA DE CUMPLEAÑOS

This entire activity is a simplified cooperative learning jigsaw. Review the process carefully with students. The entire class should brainstorm for a party theme and the kind and number of activities they feel are necessary. Remind students that in brainstorming, any and all ideas are valid. Write the suggestions on the chalkboard, on newsprint, or on an overhead transparency.

After all suggestions have been made, help students select a theme and identify an approriate number of committees. Try to organize committees so that there will be no more than five members per committee. In the jigsaw activity, each student presents his or her committee's information to the newly organized information group. Thus, the students in this second group gain information from each of the committees. Once they have this combined information, they return to their original committee and share what they have learned.

Allow ample time for the activity and circulate among students while they are working. The degree of your involvement during this activity depends on the age and developmental level of students. If your students are accustomed to cooperative learning activities, they may need less close involvement from you. You must, however, circulate among the groups and ensure that they understand and are staying on task.

Discuss **la piñata** with the class. You may wish to have students actually make a **piñata** and do the activity in class. HINT: The paper maché process is difficult and messy. Enlist the assistance of a colleague in art and have a small group of students do this as an extension activity. The **piñata** breaking activity can be boisterous and potentially hazardous. Students may tend to become overly enthusiastic and eager. Prepare them and yourself carefully for this endeavor.

J. LA FIESTA PARA ENRIQUE

Have students refer to the invitation in Activity A to answer the question ¿**A qué hora es la fiesta?** *(What time is the party?)* Answer: 8:30 in the evening. The NOTA points out a cultural factor. Discuss it with students.

Introduce **veo** and **hay**. A visual cue to **veo** is to put your hand above your eye like a visor, or to make circles with your hands to simulate eyeglasses. Practice these two vocabulary items using classroom objects or students. For example, put a number of classroom objects on a desk. Then point to them, using **veo** and **hay**. Once you have done this, ask for student volunteers to say what they see.

The food items on the table recycle some vocabulary from Element 9. Review this vocabulary by having students use their own flash cards or other forms of realia. You can incorporate the use of **veo** and **hay** as you review the vocabulary.

Allow time for students to work in pairs to identify the objects, people, and activities in the picture. The amount of time you allow will depend on the age and developmental level of students. They should write the Spanish words or phrases in the cells provided in the idea web. Do not insist on accurate spelling. This is a recognition activity. Once students have identified as much as they can, then allow them to go back to earlier Elements and make additions or necessary corrections in spelling or vocabulary.

VARIATION

Give this activity as a classwork assignment. Allow ample time for students to discuss the picture and to brainstorm aloud as much vocabulary as they can.

ASSESSMENT

Use this activity as an assessment tool. Be certain that students understand exactly what they are expected to do and on what basis they will be assessed. For example, if you are going to hold students accountable for correct spelling, then they should know this and have sufficient time to prepare.

K. MI DIARIO

By this time, students have been introduced to a considerable amount of Spanish vocabulary. Encourage them to incorporate as much of it as possible in completing the journal activity. Emphasize correct use of words and phrases over exact accuracy in spelling. Seek gradual error reduction, not complete and immediate error elimination.

The **diario** activity should foster creativity and the opportunity to experiment with new words and phrases. It is designed to be an individual effort, permitting the maximum expression of each student's linguistic and well as other talents and abilities. If you are using the **diario** as an instrument for assessment, be certain that students understand exactly how their work will be evaluated. You may wish to refer to the **Mi diario** sections in previous Elements for additional suggestions and ideas about using this activity.

13 RECUERDOS DE UN BUEN VIAJE

Special Notes to the Teacher

Remember that *¡Buen Viaje!* is intended to be an initiation to other languages and cultures. The activities in each Element focus on cultural awareness, limited second language acquisition, and the development of practical life skills.

One of the goals of *¡Buen Viaje!* is to have every student experience success in second language learning. All students are not expected to learn exactly the same content. They are, however, expected to participate in each of the activities of each Element to the level of their individual abilities. Students will demonstrate a variety and range of language proficiencies.

Element 13 is designed to address this range of proficiencies. The culminating activities offer multiple opportunities for expression. Options for using a variety of learning styles and modalities, as well as multiple cognitive approaches, are provided. To facilitate teacher assessment, an Organization and Assessment Chart has been provided as a Blackline Master (**BLM 13.4**). This Organization and Assessment Chart is meant to be only one of many methods of assessment. It may be used by both the student and the teacher as a guideline to collaboratively assess the student's work.

Levels of Assessment

Learning a language is not a linear event. Language develops globally and holistically. It is an experiential process. Watch how an infant develops his or her own first language. Observe the linguistic struggles of those individuals who have come to the United States with little or no functional ability in English. Reflect on your own experiences learning another language. Learning is most likely to occur when taking risks, using one's imagination, and being creative are encouraged. Students will manifest different levels of each of these qualities. In teaching this exploratory class, your role as a language teacher is to encourage risk taking in communicative situations. Use multiple teaching strategies and creative methods designed to enhance opportunities for communication and language learning.

Element 13 of the Student Manual gives students a format that they may use to prepare a scrapbook. It is designed as a minimal outcome for students in this course. Depending on the individual student's level of language proficiency and/or enthusiasm, you may to choose to provide students with a more independent student-generated language assessment model that uses **Recuerdos de un buen viaje** as the theme.

PERSPECTIVA

The **Perspectiva** is intended as an advance organizer to stimulate discussion about the topics to be covered in this Element. Element 13 is designed as a review of Elements 7 to 12. There are few new vocabulary items introduced in Element 13. Ask students to look at the picture of the scrapbook's title page (**BLM 13.0**). Help them recall the various topics and activities they have learned about to prepare for their imaginary homestay experience. Tell them that this Element will give them a chance to review the Spanish they have learned and to recall information they have gained about Spanish-speaking people and countries. They will review by constructing a scrapbook to show their Spanish teacher, family, and friends when they return. Emphasize that there is no single, correct, or "right" way to compile this scrapbook.

If you plan to use the Organization and Assessment Chart (**BLM 13.4**), distribute copies of the chart and discuss it with students. Be clear about your expectations regarding each of the items on the chart. Point out to students that while accuracy is always a goal, you are as concerned with their ability to use the Spanish language to function in real life situations. Note also that significant credit is given for effort and creativity.

Included below are optional assessment models that depend on the amount of time available for instruction and the student's level of language proficiency. Multiple alternative assessment models are encouraged.

Optional Model 1:

Optional Model 1 is used with students who generate language on their own or who are comfortable recombining new language and using interlanguage that has been encouraged throughout the Elements. Use the **Perspectiva** from Element 13 to set the stage for the assessment exercise. Have students develop a scrapbook without using the sentence starters. They can use the text as a review for information they choose to include. A blank scrapbook page is provided in **BLM 13.1** for students to use. Students may create an original cover using their own art design and text.

Optional Model 2:

Have students work in pairs or small groups to create a scrapbook of **recuerdos**. The group might present each area (**la familia, puntos de interés, la escuela, transportación, las compras, el consejo,** etc.) collectively. Brainstorm topics to be included in the scrapbook. Use idea mapping for brainstorming. This activity is also conducive to individual artistic expression. Students may draw pictures for the scrapbook, or they might design and decorate a group scrapbook together. They may also include a tape of their favorite music (Use **BLM 13.2** and **BLM 13.3**).

Optional Model 3:

Create a scrapbook of **una excursión** or **un viaje** that students might like to take. Encourage them to bring in pictures, posters, and travel guides of the location they have chosen. Divide students into cooperative groups. Each group chooses one of the scrapbook topics to write about, and is responsible for preparing that one section of **una excursión** or **un viaje** for the scrapbook presentation. Reserve bulletin board space to present this project.

Optional Model 4:

Plan a class party developed around the theme of a Spanish-speaking country of the students' choice. Use the party-planning model in Element 12. Have students present highlights such as music, food, or dance of the country at the party. Using a Polaroid camera or video camcorder, capture photos of the party and develop a scrapbook or video scrapbook of the preparation, presentations, and cleanup of the party. Have students write captions or a narration for the scrapbook. Students may use the format from Element 13 of the Student Manual to prepare their video scrapbook, or they may design their own video scrapbook individually, in pairs, in small groups, or as a class.

Optional Model 5:

Using computers and hypermedia, students can prepare a scrapbook on disk integrating combinations of text written on the computer, scanned pictures and photos, digitized video, and sound.